The Way of the Templar
A Manual for the Modern Knight Templar

By Timothy Hogan
Chevalier Emerys

Grand Master Order of the Temple of Secret Initiates

Copyrighted © 2015
ISBN: 978-1-329-68937-4

First English Edition 2015.

All rights reserved. No part of this book may be reproduced or transmitted in any form or by any means, electronic or mechanical, including photocopying, recording or by any information storage and retrieval system, without permission from the Publisher in writing.

© 2015 Timothy W. Hogan

***Cover painting done by Walter Stewart and Timothy W. Hogan, and based off of Templar Abraxas seal.

Index

Preface..........7

Introduction..........9

I. Little Known Templar Esoteric History..........13

II. Scottish Survival..........43

III. Larmenius Charter..........51

IV. The Rose Croix Alchemical Templar Tradition and
    the Knights of Christ..........57

V. The Germany and England Affair..........59

VI. The Society of Unknown Philosophers..........67

VII. Holy Saints John and the Johannite Gnostic Tradition..........71

VIII. Melchizadek, the Christos, the Paraclete, and the Grail.....83

IX. Living As an Expression of Templar Spiritual Chivalry..........93

X. Templar Ideas to Remember..........101

XI. Templar Collegia Proclamation..........106

XII. Recommended Reading and Sources
    Mentioned in this Book..........107

Preface

The following book is intended to provide some of the details that have been passed down from antiquity from the Templar Tradition. As such, the ideas from many lineages are presented, and much of what will be written comes from the oral history of the Templar tradition. Therefore as a warning to standard historians, ideas will be presented which may be contrary to what has come to be the standard academic teaching of historical events in schools and universities. Historians are welcome to accept or reject the claims in this book, but they are presented none the less, as the accepted accounts that are endorsed by different Templar lineages that continue to thrive to this day. Of course, the standard historian will be coming from the idea that the Templar Order was founded in 1118, grew in power and influence, and then was completely suppressed in 1307. They will acknowledge that there was an official dissolution of the Templar Order by the Roman Church on March and May of 1312, (with the Bull 'Vox in Excelso' on March 22nd, and the Bull 'Ad Providam' on May 2nd), and that with the burning at the stake of the Grand Master Jacques De Molay on March 18th of 1314, the Order ceased to exist. This book will challenge this assumption, and provide other accounts of the Templar Order founding and how the tradition has survived to our modern day. Many of the ideas presented in this book are elaborated on in my books *Revelation of the Holy Grail* and *Entering the Chain of Union*, however contained within this book is a concise history illustrating the important points to Templar history and tradition.

This book will also explore some essential philosophical ideas that this author feels, should be kept in mind by any person calling themselves a Templar. It is my belief, that if you were drawn to this book, it is because the spirit of a Templar is already within you. Without waxing too long on the doctrine of reincarnation, there are many personalities who are incarnating right now who have been received or initiated into the Templar tradition, in one manifestation or another, in ages past. They know that the work and the quest that was charged in centuries past, still holds true to this day. Others may just feel ready for this work, due to an "inner calling" in which they are drawn to it, and now is the time for their first experience of Templarism first hand.

Whether you are new or old to this work, I invite you follow the gleam and capture the spirit of Templarism- for it may be the thing that heals the wasteland that has been created by those who have come before us, and even those who live now.

Introduction

"And thus are the secrets of the heart made manifest; and so falling down on his face he will worship God, and report a truth: that God is in you." –I Cor. 14:25

The Knight Templar... the Warrior Monk... the Grail Guardian. Such images conjure thoughts in the imagination that have inspired some to the greatest acts of nobility on the one hand, and have led others into escapism or worse- into zealous fanaticism with ideas of crusading against "others" in the One Human Family. It is important, from the beginning, that in a book such as this, we clearly define what a Templar should be, and how it is relevant to our modern world.

It should be stated that there are many traditions claiming to be Templar, or claiming a Templar lineage or history. We will not dissect the different claims of the different traditions. Needless to say, some traditions have a more legitimate claim than others. Some Templar traditions are actually quite ancient, and others are more recent innovations or creations. Above all, however, regardless of what tradition or lineages a would be Templar comes from, it should be stressed, that the heart of a true Templar is found in one who desires *with all of their being* to protect the sacred- *regardless of its source*... The Templar lives by the injunction- *God first served*! The Templar understands that it is not his or her individual will which must be manifested in the world, but *Thine will be done*- the will of the Great Architect of the Universe. This is not meant in a petty sectarian sense, dependent on the false promptings of dogma from one church or religious tradition or another, in which others define what their follows need to believe, but rather from the inner promptings of the heart- from which the motivations of the Greater All can manifest according to the greater harmony of all conscious beings. *It is the light of the sacred flame within.* By its very nature then, the foundation of Templarism rests on a *Gnosis*, or a direct and personal experiential knowledge of God and the divine- regardless of what cultural names are used for this Source. *Blessed are they who live constantly in openness to the everlasting presence of God, for they shall be known as the Saviors of Humanity.* To keep this principle in mind, is to drink from the Holy Grail.

It should also be stated from the beginning, that Templar Mastery in life does not come from someone conferring a Templar title on you, but rather from the ceaseless choice to think before you act or react in all situations you encounter at any given moment of every day- in order to raise the consciousness of all situations- by transmutation. In this way, the Templar is the true social alchemist.

The Templar is first concerned with the finding the Holy area within, and then bringing this into the world around them. The Templar understands that the true Holy Land is a sacred place *that can only be found within*. It is not a territory to be fought over, or to lay claim to. A Templar must remember this: *Do not fight for a Holy Land on earth, for you will destroy the true Holy Land within...* He who is not at peace with himself is at war with the world, and he who is at peace with himself has found the true inner sanctuary, the New Jerusalem, and the Holy of Holies of the true Solomon's Temple.

The Templar is then a free agent of transmutation in the world, acting as *a working tool of the Sacred Flame within* to bring about more awakened consciousness in everyone around him or her. The mentality of most of the world when facing problems is fight or flight; but the Templar Masters understand and utilize a third option: that of transmutation. A Templar will defend the principles of personal revelation and experience- which necessitates God given Freedoms in the state, even at risk of persecution to him or herself. Consequently, the Templar must live a truly authentic life- being an embodiment of the freedom that he or she protects.

These principles being at the foundation of Templarism, it should be quite clear then, that it is not necessary for one to live in a monastery, or away from the world to be a Templar. In fact, to hide would be counter to the principle of Templarism. As the Mater Lao Tzu said, "whether one gives up all things and hides in a monastery, or goes to the other extreme and amasses great riches and a large house to shelter himself in, either way the person is not in touch with *The Way*." For a Templar is one who is disciplined in personal, spiritual practice on the one hand, while engaging in the world on the other hand. The Templar does not hide away, but rather must be open to all possibility, and consequently available to all, as opportunity demands it. This is what makes a Templar a warrior-monk. The warrior is one who engages, and is willing to sacrifice for the greater awakening of those around him or her; while the monk stays vigilant to the spiritual Source.

Keeping these fundamental principles in mind, it is my hope to explore some of the little known history of the Knights Templar, to illustrate some of the connections that Templars have fostered throughout history, and to outline what the mission is for all Templars today.

I. Little Known Esoteric Templar History

There is no need to cover here the profane Templar history as it has come down from standard historians who are looking at the manifestations of what the Order did between the years of 1118 and 1314. Rather this chapter will endeavor to reveal some little known history which helps to explain why the Order did some of the things it did in ages past. Such information, some of which is being revealed for the first time in this book, will help to explain the esoteric current that the Templars have protected and perpetuated. This chapter will cover some important details concerning the founding of the Templar Order, the end of the Order under Papal leadership and public activity, as well as some important developments in between these two points.

Exoteric history recounts how the first Grand Master of the Templar Order, Hugh de Payans, as well as Godfrey de St. Omar and seven others, all formed the Templar Order in 1118, with the stated mission to protect all of the pilgrims on their way to the Holy Land from Europe. In 1125 King Baudouin II of Jerusalem had given the title of Grand Master of the Temple to Hugh de Payans. King Baudouin II was also the one who felt that the Order needed recognition from the Pope in order to gain the necessary resources to do their stated job, (or at least get them further resources), and he therefore wrote a letter to Saint Bernard of Clairvaux asking for his help. He did this because one of the founding members of the Templar Order was Andre de Montbard, who was Bernard's uncle. Consequently, on January 13th, 1126, Hugh De Payans met with Pope Honorius' Council in Troyes, and

Saint Bernard of Clairvaux ended up writing the Rule of the Order of the Temple with 72 articles. The Templar Order assumed the early name of The Poor Knights of Christ of the Temple of Solomon. This is a quick summery of the exoteric history known to most historians. Further, it is acknowledged by historians that Bernard also helped to start the Cistercian Order, on property given to them by Hugh, Comte de Champagne, who was one of the original founding nine Templars. The name "Cistercian" comes from the fact that Bernard began his career in Citeaux, and so the monastic life that he created became known as "Cistercian". It is widely accepted that manuscripts found in the Holy Land by the Templars were given to the Cistercians to translate and record. Therefore there was a special relationship between the Templars and the Cistercians, which were both related to Bernard of Clairvaux.

Templar tradition has said that Bernard of Clairvaux was concerned with tracking down the roots of a Primordial Tradition, from which ancient knowledge could be obtained, and he was attempting to use the Templar Order and the Cistercian Order to do this. Consequently, Bernard was said to already have Druid and Albigensien Cathar leanings, as well as some Qabbalistic background, and the Templars were supposed to track down source documents related to Egyptian, Phoenician, Jewish, and other Gnostic and Apocryphal traditions, which the Cistercian Order would translate and archive. Concerning his secret Druid background, Bernard was known to have said, "Experto crede: aliquid amplius invenies in silvis, quam in libris. Ligna et lapides docebunt te, quod a magistris audire non possis", or, "Believe me, you will find more lessons in the woods than in books. Trees and stones will teach you what you cannot learn from masters".

According to *esoteric* Templar history, the Templar Order was secretly established as early as 1096 in Constantinople, primarily by another Order called the *Brothers of the East*, which itself had been established in 1057 in Constantinople by Michael Psellos. The roots of this Order of Brothers from the East, had previously come from a Pythagorean and Gnostic tradition which had resided in Greece, near Mount Olympus. In 1057, the philosopher Michael Psellos carried the fundamental elements of the Order from Greece to Constantinople, where he then became advisor to Isaac the 1st Commene, and his successors. From the beginning of his mission, Michael Psellos always worked closely with the famous Symeon Stethate, an initiate himself, and an inheritor of the wisdom of the Byzantine Corporations installed in Constantinople, and which later merged with the Order of the Brothers of the East. Michael Psellos died in 1078 at the age of 60. His successor, aged 32, took the esoteric name of Melchissedec and had the exoteric, ecclesiastical name of Theoclete, and he had assumed the head of the Order of the Brothers of the East in 1077, prior to Psellos death in 1078. He was fundamental with taking part in the events which led to the formation of the Templar Order, as plans were being made for something like the Templar Order as early as 1070. Theoclete was said to be the sixty-seventh successor of a secret Gnostic lineage of the Apostle John.

Hugh De Payans and Godfrey de Saint Omar had been sent to Constantinople after the start of the first Crusade in 1095 by Pope Urban II. They had been sent there by another secret tradition, because there was fear that the Crusading "Christian" armies would destroy and loot precious texts and artifacts known to be buried in the Holy Land or passed down by people in the region. In fact, the organization to which Hughes of Payans and Godfrey of St. Omer belonged, and which sent them to Constantinople was originally created in the 9th Century by a founder whose esoteric name was Amus, and whose exoteric name was Arnaud. Arnaud (Amus) was an advisor to Charlemagne. In the course of his traveling in the East, its founder Arnaud (hereafter called Amus), had heard of a secret society whose knowledge possessed the keys of all science and art. This society had its headquarters in Egypt. Amus was sent to Jerusalem in 778 CE to find the order and was then instructed to go to Thebes in Egypt. Amus, properly recommended, went to Thebes and was admitted into this society, which proved to be directly related to the Gnostic and Hermetic movements, and which had carried over both ancient Egyptian and Phoenician doctrines, and had been directly responsible for passing on Manichean doctrines.

From Thebes, Amus was instructed to go to Giza, where he learned great mysteries that were brought back to France. Amus is also credited with bringing the *Book of Jasher*, which he found in Jerusalem, to Europe, which is a book that had been removed from the Torah that suggests that Moses fled Egypt because of tax evasion, and that he received the Commandments not from God, but from Jethro. Studying in Egypt for two years, he then returned to France in 802 CE with the authorization to create a branch of the organization there, which was called the *"Order of the Rose Cross"*. This he did in Troyes, but its real activities began only three years later. The Egyptian source which gave him his initiation and his power resided at the area of Ros Tau- the ancient name for Giza. Needless to say, "Ros" is another name for "rose" and "tau" means "cross" in the Greek language, which was the origin of the name of the Order that Amus created, as it was the "Order from Ros Tau", or Order of the Rose Cross. There was also a military arm of this Rose Cross Order which was created at the time, which came to be known as the *Ordre des Chevaliers Faydits de la Colombe du Paraclet*, and which later had knighted Hughes Capet and many of the French line of Kings, and of which Hugh De Payans and Godfrey de Saint Omar were also received.

According to several modern Templar lineages, there was a Gnostic Adept from the areas Alexandria, Egypt, who supposedly lived in 46 CE, and was a baptized disciple of Saint Mark. He founded a kind of Christian mystery school, and the followers wore a red cross, like the priests in the initiatory tradition of Horus in Egypt. According to Templar history, when Ormus Christianized the Egyptian mysteries, he founded a new order called the Order of Ormusiens. Later, in 151 CE, the Essenes officially worked with them, since the teachings of the two groups were similar, with many Jewish traditions and doctrines originally having a root in Phoenician culture, and Christian traditions being more rooted in Egyptian culture, and of course both the Phoenicians and the Egyptians were very close in association anyway. The order then changed its name to the *Guardians of the Secret of Moses, Solomon, and Hermes*. After the fourth century, the order remained fairly small, until the twelfth century, when the order was said to have admitted Templars. It has been suggested that this Order is the same Order that Amus had created, and in fact, this is the tradition he had brought back from

Egypt, which is how it eventually came to be associated with the Templars via Hugh De Payans and Godfrey de Saint Omar.

Related to the Order of the Rose Cross created in France by Amus, there was a qabbalistic center being preserved and run in Troyes by an initiate named Shlomo Yitzhaki, and who was better known under his esoteric name as Rashi. Rashi's esoteric name came from "Rabban Shel Israel" meaning "teacher of Israel". Rashi had been initiated into the Rose Cross Order established by Amus, and was one of the leading lights within it. Rashi was born in Troyes, and he in fact likewise secretly initiated Godfrey De Bullion into this tradition, and had originally entrusted in him certain secrets regarding artifacts in the Holy Land. Rashi had also been an early tutor to Saint Bernard of Clairvaux, who wrote the first Rule for the Templar Order. In fact, this is why the first Templar Rule was 72 articles, which corresponded to the 72 Qabbalistic names of God. Some Templar traditions have also stated that this Rule was inspired from an Essenian original known as the *Rule of the Master of Justice.*

Bernard of Clairveaux had learned of Gnostic doctrines from his Uncle, Andre de Montbard, who was one of the original founders of the early Templar Order. He was also the Order's fifth Grand Master, and he was a practitioner of the Albigensian Cathar Gnosticism. It is no accident that most of the original nine Templars were vassals from the Court of Troyes, or that Chrétien of Troyes (the cousin of Hugh De Payan's wife- Catherine de St. Claire) was charged with writing aspects of the first Grail legends. These original nine knights were also largely from Albigensian Cathar families who valued and perpetuated the Gnostic wisdom deemed to also be found in qabbalistic interpretations.

Here we need to take a quick detour to discuss the Albigensian Cathars. The Albigensian Cathars were a Gnostic group in southern France that had close associations with another Gnostic group known as the Bogomils from Bulgaria, (though they also clearly had elements of Paulian Gnosticism from Armenia). As an important aside, the Albigensians were later wiped out in a Crusade by Pope Innocent III in 1147, which Bernard of Clairvaux tried to stop by praising the Cathar way of life and doctrines, but to no avail. It should be mentioned that the banner of Lord Raymond VI, Count of Toulouse, who defended the Albigensian Cathars against the armies of Innocent III, was in the form of a cross known in heraldry as *de gueules a la croix et pommettee d'Or*. In heraldry, "gueule" means "red" and was derived from the Arabic word "gul", meaning "rose". Therefore, his banner had the esoteric meaning of being a "rose cross", as related to the doctrines of the Order brought over by Amus from Giza. Lord Raymond VI died in battle and was denied burial on "holy ground" by the Roman church at the time, and so was buried in the Templar Preceptory building in Toulouse. This Preceptory building was later assumed by the Knights Hospitallier after the Templar Order was suppressed in 1307, and which later still assumed the name of the "Knights of Malta". Later still this building was turned into a hotel, where Lord Raymond's tomb resides to this day. In any event, one of the names for the Albigensian Cathars was "the Poor of Christ", and later the Templars referred to themselves as the "Poor Knights of Christ" for this reason. We are getting ahead of ourselves however! Let's return to the origin of the foundation of the Templar Order!

Hughes of Payans, the first Grand Master of the Templar Order, had originally been initiated into the Gnostic tradition from his grandfather Thibault de Payens le Maure de Gardille- who was a Moorish Sufi. Thibault had already been initiated into the Gnostic Tradition, and this involvement paved the way for Hughes of Payans initiation into the Order Rose Cross created by Amus. The Moorish Sufi tradition of Hugh De Payan's family is the reason why his original Blazon was composed of three Moor's heads, which represented his family line. (Payans, or Payens, is the same as "Pagani" in early Italian). In 1096, Hugh De Payans and Godfrey De St. Omar had already achieved important levels within the Order established by Amus, and this is why they were sent to Constantinople, and from there, ultimately on to Jerusalem.

The principle encounter which ultimately created the Templar Order at Constantinople took place in 1096, when, on the one hand, Hughes of Payans and Godfrey of St. Omer, duly mandated, met the Master Melchissedech, also known as Theoclet, of the Order of Brothers of the East, and surrounded by four officers of the Order of the Brothers of the East. Theoclet himself, had been a custodian of the Eastern Church, and as mentioned, he was secretly preserving a tradition of Johannite Gnosticism. This was very similar to the veneration of the Saints John in Albigensian Gnosticism as well, so there was great commonality when Hughes De Payans met with him for the first time. This special meeting occurred at a church called the Church of Saints Sergius and Bacchus, which was later to be called the "Little Hagia Sophia mosque", or the Küçük Ayasofya Camii in Turkish, after the Muslims took control of Constantinople. This building had originally been created by an architect named Anthemius of

Tralles, who was a mathematician and alchemist, and the author of a book on burning mirrors, called the *Paradoxographia*. The building was originally built in 527 CE.

Hugh de Payans and Godfrey de St. Omar had seven meetings at the Church of Saints Sergius and Bacchus, the second of which was dedicated to the honorary reception of Hughes of Payans and Godfrey of St. Omer into the midst of The Order of the Brothers of the East. In turn, Hughes of Payans and Godfroi of St. Omer bestowed a high honor upon the Master Melchissedech and his companions in the name of the Rose Cross Order of France. Thus a traditional exchange was established at the top levels. The ultimate result of this exchange, was that the Templar Order was created to preserve the doctrines of both traditions, which in antiquity, had come from the same source.

The Templar Order later acquired the Church of Saints Sergius and Bacchus in Constantinople where the initiations of Hughes of Payans and Godfrey of St. Omer took place, and used it as a base of operations in Constantinople for many years until the later suppression of the Templar Order in 1307. In fact, some have said that the Templar seal of two knights on one horse alludes, among other things, to both Sergius and Bacchus, and to Hughes de Payans and Godfrey of St. Omer- carrying the mission from Constantinople.

Hugh De Payans and Godfrey de St. Omar left Constantinople and within a few years, went to Jerusalem to begin their entrusted mission. According to tradition, by 1108, Hugh de Payans and Godfrey de St. Omar arrived in Jerusalem, and then began to really get things going with their Templar mission by 1111. By

1115, King Baldwin II granted them a place to reside at the area called "King Solomon's Stables", right next to the Dome of the Rock.

Everything was in place and outlined, and they merely had to follow the set plan to make the correct connections and set up operations at the area of the Dome of the Rock in Jerusalem. Due to Hugh De Payan's traditional Moorish-Sufi background, the historical record shows that the Islamic hierarchy of neither Makkah (Mecca) nor Cairo made any military or verbal move to prevent the early Templar Order from taking charge of the Dome of the Rock originally- which was regarded as the second most holy site in Islam. In fact, the Islamic records of these territories from the eleventh century on referred to the Knights Templar as "the Knights Templar of Islam". This may be due, in part, to the fact that in old Norman-French, the word "allah" means "temple". Therefore the Chevalier (or Knights) of the Temple, were likewise called the Chevalier of allah- "Allah" being the Muslim name for God. Consequently how they quickly came to be associated with knights of Islam. The Templar Order likewise possessed a "Fatwa", which is the written word of an Islamic leader (in this case that of Seville) confirming that it would be safe to let Templars take over charge of the Dome of the Rock, and it is also likely that it was these connections that allowed the early Templars to travel in various countries without attack by the Islamic leaders and their armies, as well as to land ships in safe harbors with their response of "Aleikum es salaam..". Let this fact be clear, the Templars could not have moved all the supplies and people from Europe to the Holy Land during their first 50 years of activity without having safe harbors to land ships in Islamic territories, and they could not have landed these ships without Islamic support.

The reason for the easy association between the Christian Gnostic and Qabbalistic traditions of the Rose Cross, along with the Cathars of France, and the Muslim Sufi, is owed to the fact that all of these traditions interpreted the crucifixion, death, and raising of Jesus as a metaphor, and they all likewise used the metaphor of "revelation" out of a cave or a tomb, in the matter that Plato had illustrated. They all likewise interpreted sacred scripture as metaphoric and initiatic in nature, with the Christian Gnostics focusing on the Bible and Apocryphal texts like *The Secret Questions of John*, and the Islamic Gnostics (Sufi) including the Qu'ran. Both traditions acknowledged the same Source to their doctrines however, though the transmission may have come from different prophets, or by way of different traditions. They all likewise passed down certain Hermetic, alchemical, and astrological information, which was used in their work and rituals.

In particular, these traditions were interested in certain fixed stars and the cycles that the heavens went through in relation to these fixed stars. Precisely, they were concerned with the star of Aldebaran, which was associated with Saint Michael in the heavens and Saint George on earth. To this day, many Druze Temples in Lebanon feature Saint George in their sanctuaries for this reason, and certainly these figures of Saint Michael and Saint George have been featured in the traditional Knighthood accolade "dubbing" of many Orders that have had Templar influence since 1314. The Templars, in their mission, sought to seek out other traditions that shared these philosophies, and the Druze proved to be a prime source of cooperation and mutual fellowship.

Coming from the root tradition in Egypt, at Giza, the special astrology that was being passed down by all of these traditions, focused on the three stars of Orion's belt, the five stars of the "Hyades' cluster, and the seven stars of the Pleiades, with Aldebaran directly in the center of these clusters in the sky, and hence why the shafts of the Great Pyramid align to these star systems with the capstone pointing to Aldebaran. This is also the reason why the numbers 3,5, and 7 together held significance in some of the traditions that came out of the Templars.

From the very beginning of the Templar Order, we therefore see elements and influence of Gnosticism, Qabbalistic thought, Sufism, Druidism, astrological and alchemical doctrines, and these philosophies added further fuel to their work and mission in the years to come, and their connections with diverse groups like the Druze, Jewish, Muslim, Yazidi, Mithraic, and Coptic communities. The original mission of the Templars then became the job of seeking out and rescuing from annihilation, the secret doctrines protected by these schools of thought in Europe, Northern Africa, and the Middle East, all the time while the Crusades were raging in these areas. At the same time, the Templars had to assume the external mantle of the Roman Catholic doctrine that outwardly originally gave the Templar Order its Rule and initial funding...

Accordingly, the Templar Order passed on these doctrines and connected with other groups within the Gnostic Tradition. As mentioned, one such group they connected with especially was the Tawhid Muwahadoon, also called commonly the "Druze". The Druze Gnostics celebrated the traditions of Plato, Pythagoras, and Hermes, as well as prophets from the Bible, and even from the Qu'ran. They were and are, essentially Unitarian Gnostics.

Let us explore a possible connection between the Druze and the Templars. In the following, I will mostly summarize some important points made by researcher Jean-Pierre Schmit in his excellent article *The Secret Statutes of the Knights Templar*, and found on the website Les Fils de la Vall`ee. There is a series of documents first published in 1877 by Theodore Merzdorff, which were said to come from the Masonic Grand Lodge of Hamburg. These Latin documents were the official Rule of the Knights Templar followed by three other documents said to be secret statutes of the Order. They were said to be copies of original documents that had existed in the Vatican, which were copied in the 1780s-1790s by the Danish scientist Frederic Münter. The documents were translated into German, and from there into French in 1957 by Rene Gilles. The documents consisted of the following:

- The official Templar Rule, composed of the seventy-two articles, with seven articles complementing the 'Regula' dated on St. Felix's feast day, 1205, and transcribed by brother Matthew Tramlay. This rule is similar to other known copies of the Knights Templar Rule.

- The second document dated August 1252 beginning with "Here begin the secret statutes of the Elected Brothers " consists of thirty articles approved by two dignitaries of the order, Roger de Montagu, Preceptor of Normandy, and Robert de Barris, Procurator.

- The third document dated July 1240 opens with "Here begins the" liber consolamenti "or secret statutes, written by Master Roncelinus for the Consoled Brothers of the militia of the

Temple". These statutes, composed of twenty articles are signed by Master Roncelinus and another dignitary of the Templar Order, brother Robert of Samford, Procurator of the Knights Templar in England.

- The last piece dated August 1240 starts with: "Here begins the list of secret signs that master Roncelinus has assembled in eighteen articles and addressed to the same Robert of Samford."

Since these documents had come from a Masonic Grand Lodge, had been copies of copies, and were not original documents, there was originally great suspicion from scholars as to their authenticity at the time they were published, which somewhat persists to the current day. However a reexamination of the documents in light of recent known history of the Templars has shed possible new light on their authenticity. What interests us from a Druze standpoint, is that the Druze are mentioned in these documents, but since it was never believed in the 1800s that there had been associations with Druze during the Crusades, such mentions were previously dismissed. We now know, for example, that a medieval Jewish traveler named Benjamin of Tudela (1130-1173) made a pilgrimage to the Holy Land between 1163 and 1173 and he described the customs of the Druze in his *The Travels of Benjamin* (בנימין מסעות, Masa'ot Binyamin, also known as ספר המסעות, Sefer ha-Masa'ot, The Book of Travels), thereby demonstrating that pilgrims were cataloguing Druze at this early date, and that the name "Druze" was in use by pilgrims at the time that these statutes were said to have been written originally. The assumption that European pilgrims did not actually know the Druze by this name back then can thereby be thrown out.

There is also a Roncelinius who is mentioned in the statutes, and it was assumed that this name was taken from the testimonies of Templar trials between 1307 and 1314 that mentions a similar name. Since the document mentioned both Druze and a name that had been assumed to be borrowed, the text was thought to be a made up forgery by some historians. However recent historians have determined that there was a master Roncelin in the Templar order at the estimated period of writing of the statutes, and he was stationed in the territory of Tripoli, thereby possibly reestablishing its legitimacy. Debate will likely continue to happen on whether the documents came from a legitimate source, however to weigh in favor of their possible legitimacy, we cannot ignore the fact that Templar traditions and the Druze themselves have always insisted on these associations, and it is interesting that these claims appeared in documents published in 1877, and were said to have been taken from the archives of a Masonic Grand Lodge prior to that, and were said to have come from copies made in the 1780s. This shows, at the very least, that there were Masonic traditions claiming a Templar-Druze connection as early as the 1780s, if we are to accept the fact that these were indeed originally produced at that time. Since this book will not solve the debate one way or another, (and may in truth only add more fuel to the fire), and since modern Templar lineages agree with the assertions in the documents, let us go ahead and look at a couple sections from the Articles of the *Secret Templar Statutes*:

In Article 8 of the *Rule of the Consoled Brothers* of 1240, we read:

"There are Elected brothers and Consoled brothers throughout the world. Where you see tall buildings built, make the signs of recognition and you will find many righteous men, with the knowledge of God and of the Great Art. They have received it from their fathers and masters and are all brothers. Among them are: the Good Men of Toulouse, the Poor of Lyon, the Albigensian, those near Verona and Bergamo, the Bajole of Galicia and Tuscany, the Beghards and Bulgarians. You will lead them to your chapters by underground passages and for those who are fearful, you will give them the Consolamentum outside the chapter before three witnesses. "

And in Article 9 of the *Comforted Brothers* : "you will receive fraternally the Brothers of these groups and, in the same way, the Consoled of Spain and Cyprus will fraternally receive the Saracens, the Druze and those who live in Lebanon."

Immediately we recognize not only special associations with the territories associated with Gnostic activity, like the Albigensian Cathars, and who were active in Toulouse), and the Bulgarians (who had the Gnostic sect of the Bogomils), but we also see a special relationship with the Druze of Lebanon. The Templar Provincial House of Tortosa was located at the border of the territories controlled by the Muslim Ismaili sect of the Assassins, which was founded around 1090 by Hassan Sabah, and is thought to have had close relations with the Sufi. (The Ismaili sect has long been suspected of Manichean Gnostic foundations). In fact, there is strong evidence to suggest that the levels of organization of the Templars was nearly identical to that of the Assassins, and may have even been modeled after them. Throughout the twelfth century, this sect paid a tribute of two thousand bezants to the Templars, which an emissary brought annually to the Templar House of Tortosa. It is in these same Lebanese mountains overlooking the County of Tripoli that one would expect to encounter the Druze. Roncelin de Fos, having been Master of the Province of Tripoli, was bound to know them and it is hardly surprising that he was listed as writing Article 9 of the *Comforted Brothers*. This suggests that there were indeed associations between the Druze and the Templars at this early date, and it may also explain why the Masonic Grand Lodge of Hamburg had an interest in this at such an early date.

To add further evidence to the secret Gnostic tradition found at the foundation of the Templars, the Templars were likewise known for using the Gnostic talisman of Abraxas on certain seals, and it was once found carved on the floor of their castle at Acre, Israel, (but has hence been removed in recent years by "authorities"). Abraxas was a rooster-headed figure that represented time, the stages of initiation, and the divisions of consciousness awareness within the body. Abraxas has a rooster head, as a rooster heralds in the new light of the day with its cry. Abraxas, according to Gnostic myth, was originally an Archon, (or guardian who kept people from spiritually evolving towards enlightenment until they were ready), and who, after seeing the light of God, had attained true Gnosis, and left the life of keeping people enslaved to a false reality, so to speak. He has been called the "son of Sophia"- along with Sophia's other children which have traditionally been labeled "Faith, Hope, and Charity". In some depictions, Abraxas is also featured with the head of the lion and the body of a serpent, or in other words, he started out crawling on the ground, close to the earth, but later through revelation he became a lion- or full of the vigor of the true life of understanding, and a philosophical king that reigned over attachment to the earth. He is regularly depicted with seven stars next to him, representing the seven centers of consciousness awareness in the body and the seven planets of antiquity, as well as the letters IAO, which was the secret Gnostic name for God.

Above Left: Abraxas as a lion-headed serpent. Above Right: Abraxas as a rooster from an old Templar seals.

Along with the Gnostic tradition of the Templars, there were certain alchemical doctrines that the Templars utilized in their ceremonies and rituals, as well as for healing. It is no coincidence that the Templars were known for using certain mold extracts for healing purposes, which were in reality an early form of antibiotics. Nor is it coincidence that they developed CPR- which was tied to the life force principle called "mercury" in alchemy, which could reanimate and bring consciousness to the lifeless body. This mercury force was said to reside in the air.

To cite one historical episode in the alchemical history of the Templars, in 1245 William de Sonnac became the Sovereign Grand Master of the Templar Order in Jerusalem. Later, in 1247, Brother William de Sonnac, sent a distinguished Knight Templar delegation to England, in order to present to King Henry III 'a portion of the Blood of our Lord, which He shed to the Cross with the salvation with the planet, enclosed in the handsome crystalline vessel.' This was intended to win further cooperation between the Templar Order and King Henry III in England. The relic was authenticated beneath seal from the Patriarch of Jerusalem, the bishops, abbots and nobles on the Holy Land. The sacred vessel was called the "Chalice of the Rose Cross", (from the tradition that Amus had brought to France that the Templars were passing on). It contained a rare hermetic and alchemical elixir, which was called the "Blood of Christ" or the "Red Lion". This vessel passed into the possession of Henry IV, King of Navarre- who was a knight of the Ordre des Chevalier Faydits de la Colombe du Paraclet, and Grand Master of the Ordre de Saint Michael in France. The vessel and its contents were later deposited in the cathedral church of St. Paul.

Within the work of the Templars should also be mentioned the Compagnons of the middle ages, which are widely accepted as being the cathedral builders of France. This group had, in fact, started out as part of the building work force of the Templars, and had continued to be partnered and protected by the Templars throughout the middle ages. In fact, most of the cathedral funding came from Templar money secured from out of France, and this is why, when the Templars were later suppressed, the cathedral building age came to an end. The Templar mason division is mentioned in the Templar Rule of 1268, in which it says the following in section #325 as to their right to wear leather gloves:

- "No brother should ever swear when angry or calm, nor should he ever say an ugly or vile word, even less do such a thing. Each brother is required to do all noble actions and say all good words. No brother should wear leather gloves, except the chaplain brothers who are permitted to wear them in honour of Our Lord's body, which they often hold in their hands; and the (Templar) Mason brothers may wear them sometimes...but they should not wear them when not in work."

The mention of the Compagnons by name first appears in the 1420 ordinance of Charles VI, though tradition had acknowledged them as existing previously in the 1100s on. Derived from the Compagnons were the building guilds of the *Children of Solomon* and *Children of the Mater Jacques*. These guild traditions exist to this day, and according to them, they both came from the Templars. In fact, the "Children of Solomon" just got their name from the "Children of the Poor Knights of the Temple of Solomon", or Templars, and the Children of the Master Jacques got their name from Jacques De Molay, the Grand Master who had been burnt at the stake in 1314.

Within the many gothic cathedrals of France can be found the signatures of the Templars. These include the repetitious painting of the Templar cross, as found in places like Saint Germaine cathedral in Paris; the alchemical knowledge depicted in statuary and carvings in cathedrals like Chartres, Notre Dame du Paris, and Amiens; the stained glass windows which were made with metallic oxides that required metallurgy alchemical knowledge; the fact that when viewed from the air the cathedrals are in the shape of a cross and they have rose windows in them, thus making them "rose crosses"; the use of the black and white checkered pavements in these cathedrals, as related to the Templar flag; the carvings and depictions of Templars themselves on these cathedrals- as for example two Templars being depicted holding a shield and representing the constellation of Gemini on one of the outside arches at Chartres cathedral; and finally the fact that the cathedrals of Notre Dame were built as giant human bodies in stone, so that when one leaves the arch, or opening of the cathedral, one is born from Notre Dame, "our Lady", as the Christ- which was a completely Gnostic concept not accepted or understood by the Roman church at the time. Also within many of the cathedrals like Chartres and Amiens are labyrinths, in which one takes the "internal journey" to get to Jerusalem- the "New Jerusalem", the sacred place within- which was likewise a Gnostic idea. At least one of these cathedrals, Saint Germaine in Paris, (which was the oldest cathedral in Paris), was likewise built on an old Egyptian Temple dedicated to Isis.

Above Left- Carving of a person pulling a salamander out of an alchemical Athenor oven at Amiens cathedral.
Above Right- Carving of Pythagoras at Chartres Cathedral.

Templar tradition has suggested that the Templar Order accomplished its mission of rescuing certain artifacts and documents from the Holy Land. In fact, traditional qabbalistic teaching has maintained that the Templar Order managed to retrieve the original *Zohar* and *Sephir Ha'Bahir* from Jerusalem, and that these were later given to Jewish communities in Spain. The Zohar was then published by the same printers who published *Parzival* by Wolfram von Eschenbach for the first time. In fact, Rabbi David Joseph Hayim Azulai (1755) records the following:

"Based on ancient Jewish records, the Zohar was found in the Land of Israel by Moslem workers who were serving Christian (Templar) masters. A Moslem worker unearthed some clay jars, inside of which were some ancient scrolls. The worker then took the scrolls to his Christian master who could not decipher them. The Christian master then went to a local, but trusted Rabbi who was indeed able to recognize and decipher the scrolls, and thus the Zohar was discovered. The scrolls were then smuggled out of the Holy Land in Jewish hands who travelled on a Templar ship. They made their way to Spain and into the hands of Rabbi Moshe DeLeon. It is allegedly he who then transcribed the scrolls and published the Zohar."

Not only were there these Jewish associations with the Templars, but there is a little known fact of "lost history" that the Egyptian Sultan General Saladin, who was head of the Muslim armies, was actually knighted into the Order of the Knights Templar, ca. 1190 AD. One 13th century manuscript, the French work called "Ordene de Chevalerie" ("Order of Chivalry") written ca. 1250 AD, historically documented an event in which Saladin was given and received the secret induction ceremony of the Knights Templar.

The annals of the history of the Crusades in Jerusalem likewise records the story of a young Frankish Knight entering the Dome of the Rock and being met with a Muslim praying towards Makkah. Losing his temper, he intimidated the Muslim who was praying "the wrong way". The Frankish Knight then found himself taken to task by two Knights Templar who ordered him out of the holy precinct, and told him not to come back until he had learned "manners and tolerance". The Templars then, on behalf of the expulsed knight, apologized to the Muslim for the Frank's misgiving attitude. Ignoring directives from Rome, the Templars gave all Muslims and Jews the right to pray in their own way in Jerusalem.

These episodes, along with many other examples, illustrate that the Templars were not mere crusaders who were attempting to pull Jerusalem away from Muslim control. It is true that they got pulled into fighting on many occasions during their stay in Jerusalem, but their purpose there far transcended what standard historians have suggested.

This brings us to the famous suppression of the Templar Order on Friday, October 13th, 1307, and the ultimate burning at the stake of the Order's Grand Master Jacques De Molay in 1314. Most historians are quick to suggest that all the Templars in France were rounded up in one swift move and the Order was suppressed quickly thereafter, never to exist again. However this is a major simplification of what really happened. Indeed, 620 Templars were rounded up in Paris, (of the 3000+ that resided there), in the weeks following October 13th, 1307, and those captured were interrogated and many were tortured for years afterward, and made to confess to all kinds of fabricated things in order for King Phillip IV (the Fair) of France to justify seizing property and assets of the Templar Order. The Roman Church at the time was complacent with this scheme, due to pressure by Philip and concern about the Templar recognition of spiritual traditions and doctrines outside of the Roman Church. Ultimately the Grand Master Jacques De Molay was burnt at the stake in March of 1314. The Order was declared illegal by the state and no longer sanctioned by the Church via two Papal Bulls in March and May 1312. After the "Providam Bull", issued on May 2nd, 1312, all Templar properties were transferred to a rival Order, the Knights Hospitallier, (who later became known as the Knights of Malta), thereby ensuring that property remained in Roman church hands. Indeed, prior to the persecution, Pope Clement V and Philip the IV were attempting to get the Templar Order to merge with the Hospitallier Order, of which Phillip had hoped to assume the title of "Rex Bellator", or "war king", thus having the resources to fund the wars he was hoping to wage. As far as what the profane outside world thought, this was the end of the Templar Order.

Even though most historians assert, in error, that it was a complete surprise to the Order that they were going to be suppressed, I can state emphatically, based on the records and oral history of the Templar Order lineage that I represent, that there were Templar leaders who knew the suppression was coming weeks ahead of time! The arrest orders had been issued by Philip IV on September 14th, 1307, almost a full month before the actual arrests, and the Templars had allies at the highest levels of Philip's court who were able to secretly alert the Grand Master Jacques DeMolay to what was issued. King Philip had called DeMolay to Paris in the autumn of 1307 to keep him close at hand, and DeMolay went in order to not betray the fact that he knew an attack was imminent. In fact, the day before the raids, DeMolay acted as pallbearer for King Philip's sister-in-law. In the four weeks before the suppression, most of the Templar assets, artifacts, relics, and treasures were secretly moved to new, safe, and hidden places- many gradually taken by 18 ships from the port of La Rochelle. While 4/5th of the Templars were able to subtly go into hiding, or travel to safe places to regroup, 1/5th of the Templars stayed behind with DeMolay to give an appearance that "all was business as usual", and to not alert authorities as to what was being smuggled out of the country of France.

Templars were then able to assume new identities, in new places, while still staying true to the Order in secret. Thus while in some areas they merged into other Knighthood Orders of the time, like the Teutonic and Hospitlallier Orders, in other areas they assumed the guise of stone masons or other guilds. Some Templars even went back to the Holy Land areas and converted to Islam and became Sufi, or became members of Druze communities who they already had close relationships with. Some Templars went on to serve in armies for independence in other countries. Some Templars even sailed to areas in the Americas, of which there had already been secret Templar bases established. (Researchers interested in this possibility are directed towards the Newport Tower in Rhode Island, the Kinsington Rune Stone in Minnesota, and the white Indians of Darien known as the "Chepu Tules" in Panama). Through the sacrifice of a few, the many were able to get to safety and protect the treasures and secret doctrines of the Order. There are even legends of some Templar fleets disappearing, only to become the first pirate ships.

DeMolay had hoped that while voluntarily being arrested, he could influence the arrestors to free the Order and drop all charges, while at the same time, he could buy time for those who were escaping to other territories. This brings us to the true sacrifice of DeMolay and the other 619 Templars who were rounded up. These brave souls voluntarily sacrificed themselves for a greater cause, and to protect the rest of their Templar brothers and sisters. They stayed behind knowing that they would be arrested, and likely tortured and killed for being Templars! I am sure they had hoped that events would have turned out better and in their favor, but as it turned out, things turned for the worst. The Order was suppressed and had to go underground, and its highest leadership had been burned at the stake! Since it was known ahead of time that suppression was going to take place, great care was taken and planned as to what the possible outcomes would be. As such, there was a plan already in place, as to what prospects could replace DeMolay as Grand Master, should the worst case scenario occur, and he be executed.

When the Templars left Palestine in 1187, the teachings of the early Rose Cross tradition of Amus were spread throughout the rest of Europe. The alchemist Raymond Lully was admitted into the order, and Templar tradition has claimed that Raymond Lully was a Templar, (though he operated more as a secret agent of the Templars), not publically showing himself as a Templar. Historically, it is known that Raymond Lully was a Catalan monk, born in 1232. He was present, officially, as a member of the

Roman Church at the abolition of the Templar Order at the Council of Vienne. Lully did not attempt to intervene on the Templars behalf however, as he determined that he could better help to influence things in other ways during the Templar operation of hiding. He was known for attempting to suggest for the unification of the Templar Order with the Knights Hospitallier, in order to continue to protect its work, but Jacques De Molay was firmly opposed to the merger. Lully was known to have acquired many of his alchemical doctrines from the Sufi and the Druze of the Middle East, and from the Templar associations between these groups.

In the next few chapters, we will explore a few of the places that the Templar Order went after its suppression, according to various Templar traditions. We will not be able to explore all of the theories, as Templars fled all over the place after persecution. Therefore we will not cover in any detail the accounts of some Templars merging into other Orders like the Hospitallier of Saint John Order, the Teutonic Order, the strong tradition of their fleeing to areas of Switzerland and Norway, and their conversions to other faiths in other countries to survive. We will explore where they continue to have the strongest expressions.

Above Left: Saint Bernard of Clairvaux
Above Right: Early Payans/Pagani Coat of Arms

Above Left: Sufi Alchemical Manuscript from Middle ages
Above Right: Person holding a shield with a salamander on it at Notre Dame du Paris.

Above: Alchemical book plate from the 1500s showing the origins of the alchemical tradition. The first person listed is Michael Psellos, who helped to establish the Templar Order in Constantinople. Also included are various Arab alchemists, which had come from the Sufi and Druze traditions that the Templars had been in contact and working with.

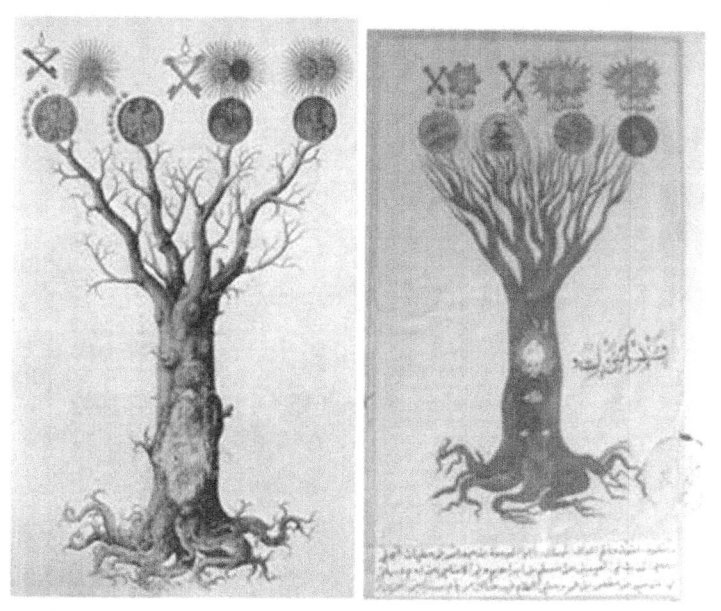

Above Left: Raymond Lully Alchemical Diagram. Above Right: Original Sufi diagram that Lully got the diagram from, currently residing in the OTSI archives.

Above: Early image of Michael Psellos and Byzantine Emperor Michael VII Doukas.

Above left: Jacques DeMolay   Above Right: Templar seal

Above Left: Druze Sheik in Lebanon. Above Right: Templar Druid Ray Hayward.

II. The Scottish Survival

Traditions have persisted that when the Templars were suppressed, many fled to Scotland and helped excommunicated King Robert the Bruce fight the Scottish war of independence against the British King Edward I.

It is said that due to their help, the Templars were absorbed into the Order of Saint Andrew, and were later incorporated into the Royal Order of Scotland, in which the knighthood title is a Knight of the Rosy Cross of Kilwinning. The symbolism of "Rosy Cross" is again tied to the tradition that Amus had developed. Templars in Scotland were also later absorbed into the Order of the Thistle. Masonic tradition has remained adamant over the centuries that it was also at this point in history in which Freemasonry was really established as an order in Scotland for Templars on the run. This hypothesis has been explored independently by many historians, some of the best books on the subject being *Born in Blood*, by John J. Robinson, and *The Temple and the Lodge*, by Michael Baigent and Richard Leigh, and *The Warriors and the Bankers*, by Alan Butler and Stephen Dafoe.

Templar graves have been discovered in Scotland, at a graveyard in Argyllshire, dating from the early 1300s, and, as the centuries moved forward, these same gravestones demonstrated an evolution of symbols such as Templar swords, the Grail, and Masonic implements becoming Masonic implements only, and being used by families passing on the tradition. The skull and crossbones also show up on these grave stones in the 1300s, and are later associated with the third degree, or Master Mason degree in Freemasonry. This symbol had been used early on by the Templars, as in heraldry, when a person was depicted at death with crossed legs, it meant that they had served in the Holy Land. Robinson clearly demonstrates that the first three degrees of Freemasonry, which are usually associated with the building of Solomon's Temple, are actually associated with the Poor Knights of Christ of the Temple of Solomon, or Templars. This hypothesis claims that the Templars traded in their lambskin tunics for lambskin aprons, and adopted the practice of building cathedrals. (The Templars previously had built over 100 Gothic chapels and cathedrals in less than 200 years of outward activity). This has also been suggested as one of the reasons why Jacques de Molay and his Norman Preceptor Geoffrey de Charney were burned at the stake in front of Notre Dame Cathedral.

The higher degrees of Masonic ritual have suggested a Templar connection for centuries, but Masons have chosen not to reveal this information to an often cruel and misinformed public, and in recent years, there have been so called "Masonic experts", who have chosen to believe that the whole Templar tradition in Freemasonry was just the whimsical imaginings of Masons in the late 1700s, without any history to back it up. Albert Pike, often considered the philosophical father of Scottish Rite Freemasonry, stated in his 1871 edition of *Morals and Dogma*:

"The end of the Drama [of the Templars] is well known, and how Jacques de Molai and his fellows perished in flames. But before his execution, the Chief of the doomed Order organized and instituted what afterward came to be called the Occult, hermetic, or Scottish Masonry. In the gloom of his prison, the Grand Master created four Metropolitan Lodges, at Naples for the East, at

Edinburgh for the West, at Stockholm for the North, and at Paris for the South. The initials of his name, J.B.M., found in the same order in the first three degree (pass words of Freemasonry), are but one in the many internal and cogent proofs that such was the origin of modern Free-Masonry."

Of relevance to Albert Pike's quotation is the fact that one of the secret Templar lodges was said to be established at Edinburgh, near the location of the famed Rosslyn Chapel, which has carved within it scenes of Templar initiation which are similar to Freemasonry, as well as foliage that can only be found in the "new world" of the Americas, even though the chapel was completed by 1420- which was 72 years before Columbus was said to have discovered America. Also within the chapel are carved geometric images on blocks, above angels playing instruments, which have been found to be Cymatic music designs. These carvings are found in only one other place from the time of the Templars, and that is underneath the ledges of the former Templar Commandery in Istanbul, known as the Church of Saints Sergius and Bacchus, which was later to be called the "Little Hagia Sophia mosque", or the Küçük Ayasofya Camii in Turkish. This was the place where the Brothers of the Orient resided, and where Hughes De Payans and Godfrey De Saint Omar were given the mandate to start the Templar Order. If this were not enough, the former Templar Commandery in Istanbul was built like a giant bee hive, and Rosslyn Chapel had the first and only operational working bee hive in Europe, which had been carved into a building, and which rests on the roof of the chapel. The symbol of the bee hive later became important in masonic ritual, even though the United Grand Lodge of England no longer uses it in their ritual work.

The oldest surviving Masonic minutes date from 1599 in Edinburgh and the oldest Masonic Lodge room still in use is at the Canongate Kilwinning Lodge No. 2. As early as 1491, Edinburgh authorities allowed their masons to "get a recreation in the commoun luge." The Masonic "Word" appears in Scotland around 1550 and there were twenty-five Scottish lodges operating before the public announcement of Freemasonry on Saint John the Baptist day of 1717.

Other researchers have pointed out that the York *Regius Manuscript* of 1390 makes mention of the Masons, in relation to defining English law. The manuscript states:

"This craft came into England, as I tell you, in the time of good king Athelsan's reign; he made both hall, and also bower and lofty temples of great honor, to take his recreation in both day and night, and to worship his God with all his might. This good lord loved this craft full well, and purposed to strengthen it in every part on account of various defects that he discovered in the crafeet He sent out into all the land, after all the Masons of the craft, to come straight to him, to amend all these defects by good counsel, if it might so happen. He then permitted an assembly to be made of divers lords in their ranks, dukes, earls, and barons, also knights, squires and many more, and the greatest burgesses of that city, they were all there in their degree; these were there, each one in every way to make laws for the state of these Masons. There they sought by their wisdom how they might govern it; there they found out fifteen articles, and there they made fifteen points."

The document also suggests that the tradition originally came from Egypt, and it is interesting to note that King Athelsan resided in England around the same time that Amus had brought the Rose Cross tradition to France, from Egypt. Further, we mentioned the 15 fixed stars especially venerated by the Rose Cross tradition, which were also called "points" in astrology, and this may be the origin of the 15 points in the Regius Manuscript of 1390.

John J. Robinson also goes on to show that it was the work of these same underground Templars that stirred up the Peasant Revolt in England. This revolt led to the establishment of common people's rights in England. These revolts were at the time said to be organized by a "Great Secret Society," all the signs of which point to organized fugitive Templars who had established the early mason guilds, and were attempting to get back some of their possessions which had been seized by the Knights Hospitallier after the Templar suppression.

It is interesting to point out the Masonic belief that the Order of the Temple possessed a great secret, related to the Grail, which also contained a Gnostic and Hermetic philosophy similar to that of the Cathars, and was believed to even have connection to the Essenes. Albert Pike again hints at this in his *Morals and Dogma*, when he says:

"The Templars...took as their models, in the Bible, the Warrior-Masons of Zorobabel, who worked, holding the sword in one hand and the trowel in the other. Therefore it was that the Sword and the Trowel were the insignia of the Templars...The secret thought of Hughues de Paynes, in founding his Templar Order, was not exactly to serve the ambition of the Patriarchs of Constantinople.

There existed at that period in the East a Sect of Johannite Christians, who claimed to be the only true initiates of the religion of the Saviour. They pretended to know the real history of Yesus the Anointed, and, they held that the facts recounted in the Evangels are but allegories, the key of which Saint John gives...The Johannites ascribed to Saint John the foundation of their Secret Church, and the Grand Pontiffs of the Sect assumed the title of Christos, and claimed to have succeeded one another from Saint John by an uninterrupted succession of pontifical powers. He who, at the period of the foundation of the Order of the Temple, claimed these prerogatives, was named Theoclet; he knew Hughes de Payens, he initiated him into the mysteries and hopes of his church...and finally designated him as his successor. Thus, the Order of the Knights of the Temple was at the very origin devoted to the cause of opposition to the tiara of Rome and the crowns of Kings, and the Apostolate of Kabalistic Gnosticism was vested in its chiefs. For Saint John himself was the Father of the Gnostics...The Chiefs alone knew the (true) aim of the Order: the Subalterns followed them without distrust. To acquire influence and wealth, then to intrigue, and at need to fight, to establish the Johannite or Gnostic and Kabalistic dogma, were the object and means proposed to the initiated Brethren. The Templars, like all other Secret Orders and associations, had two doctrines, one concealed and reserved for the Masters, which was Johannism; the other public, which was the Roman Catholic. Thus they deceived the adversaries whom they sought to supplant. Hence Freemasonry, adopting Saint John the Evangelist as one of its patrons...[can proclaim itself] the child of the Kabalah and Essenism together."

Pike also writes:

"The [Templar] Order disappeared at once. Its estates and wealth were confiscated, and it seemed to have ceased to exist. Nevertheless it lived, under other names and governed by unknown chiefs, revealing itself only to those who, in passing through a series of degrees, had proven themselves worthy to be entrusted with the dangerous Secret...The successors of the Ancient Adepts Rose-Croix, abandoning by degrees the austere and hierarchal Science of their Ancestors in initiation, became a Mystic Sect, united with the Templars, the dogmas of the two intermingling, and believing themselves to be the sole depositories of the secrets of the Gospel of Saint John, seeing in its recitals an allegorical series of rites proper to complete the initiation."

Currently the Scottish Rite, York Rite, Swedish Rite, and Rectified Scottish Rite of Freemasonry all perpetuate Templar degrees in which they discuss Templar philosophy and tradition from different perspectives.

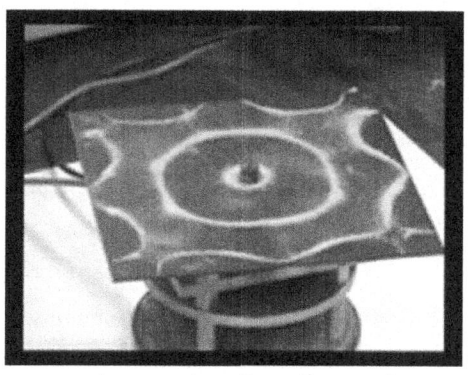

Above Left: Templar Initiation carved at Rosslyn Chapel in Scotland
Above Right: Depiction of cymatic music designs with sand on a vibrating plate, using modern equipment to make them

Above: Cubes at Rosslyn Chapel with Cymatic music designs on them
Above Photos by Thomas J. Mitchell

Above: "Little Hagia Sophia" mosque, which was the former Templar Commandery in Constantinople, and base for the Brothers of the East, where cymatic music designs are carved under the ledges that are similar to the ones at Rosslyn chapel in Scotland.

III. Larmenius Charter

There are certain Templar lineages that claim their roots from a document called the *Charter of Transmission of Larmenius*, usually known as the Larmenius Charter. These groups include, but are not limited to, the Order of the Temple of Secret Initiates (OTSI)- a worldwide lineage whose headquarters is currently in the United States; the Ordre Secret du Temple (OST), located in Cordes (formerly called Tarn) France, and which has close ties with the OTSI; Sion, which operates from Switzerland; the Supremus Militaris Templi Heirosolymitani; and the Ancient and Military Order of the Temple of Jerusalem, which operates from Portugal, though it started in France. (The last two Orders are more fraternal societies with Christian chivalry leanings, while the first groups listed tend to promote the alchemical and Gnostic doctrines as mandated at the beginning of the Templar Order).

This charter was said to have been written in 1324 by Johannes Marcus Larmenius, who was appointed Grand Master by Jacques de Molay himself while de Molay was imprisoned. The scroll bears the signatures of all of the subsequent Grand Masters of the underground Templar Order, which is significant because, according to most historians, after the execution of Jacques de Molay, there were not supposed to be any others. The Templars coming from this Charter began to go somewhat public in 1804 through Dr. Bernard Raymond Fabré-Palaprat (better known by his esoteric name, Fabré-Palaprat), who was the Grand Master of the Templar Order in France at the time.

History records that as early as 1451, there were Templar Priories who had received a new RULE, and the Archbishop of Reims, Robert de Lenoncourt, became Grand Master in 1478. With this choice of Grand Master there was an attempt at a rapprochement, or reconciliation with the Vatican for a possible restoration of The Order, but to no avail.

Likewise, Philippe, Duke of Orleans, was Templar Grand Master, and he had convened a General Convent at Versailles in 1705. It was during the course of this Convent that the General Statutes were presented. They were based upon the Templar Rule, which had been recognized in 1128 for the Templar Order at the Council of Troyes. They were drawn up in Latin. In 1747 and 1779, Louis-Francois de Bourbon, Prince of Conti, and Louis-Hercule-Timoleon of Cosse, Duke of Brissac, each as Grand Master on the dates indicated on the Larmenius Charter, sought again to reconcile with Rome in order to have annulled the decision of the Council of Vienne taken in 1313.

So when Dr. Bernard Raymond Fabre Palaprat announced the Templars coming forward again in 1804, it really wasn't the new tradition that some people have made it out to be.

Many historians have tried to dismiss the Larmenius Charter as a forgery or hoax, basing their objections on a nineteenth-century translation of the original Latin. (The original document was written in a code based on the geometry of a Templar cross). To quote Picknett and Prince in their book *The Templar Revelation*: "One of the reasons it has been dismissed as a forgery is that the Latin is too good for the time—medieval Latin being notoriously haphazard—but in fact the translator had corrected the grammar.

The critics have also dismissed the list of the declarations of Grand Masters because the form of words for each one is exactly the same, something that is unlikely over the time span of 1324-1804. But again this is simply because the transcriber standardized them: in the original they were all different. So the two main reasons for rejecting the Larmenius Charter do not, in fact, hold water." This being the case, there is no reason to suppose that the Larmenius Charter is a forgery. Most people simply look *at the translation* of the Larmenius Charter, as was done in 1804, and which now resides at Mark Mason's Hall in London, and mistake it for the original charter. The original charter, as done in the Templar cypher code, was last known to have been given to Count Szapary on July 23, 1857, who was the Grand Prior in Paris, along with other archives. The archives and the Charter, contained in four large cases, were sent to Mr. Maury, Director General of the National Archives (in Paris), their arrival being signaled by a letter from Dr. Vernois, dated August 15, 1871, which itself is now in the National Archives in Paris. From there, the original charter in the Templar cypher code had disappeared into unknown obscurity!

The Charter also had on it an early criticism against the "Scot-Templars deserters" written by Larmenius himself, as well as a criticism of the Hospitalliers of St. John of Jerusalem, (likely for assuming the Templar property after the persecution). This is significant, as public information proving the evolution of Freemasonry from Scottish Templars has only recently come to light. Historians of the past have dismissed the Larmenius Charter as a forgery trying to compete with Scottish Freemasonry (which first claimed such roots in 1750). The Larmenius Charter's authenticity would indicate knowledge of the Templar-Scotland-Freemasonry connection as early as 1324, and is alluded to by the information in the last chapter. The two Templar lineages from France and from Scotland have no resentment for each other, and there is even evidence to suggest that the Chevalier Ramsay (who first publicly announced that Freemasonry came from the Templars in the 1700s) may have received his information from this underground Templar body in France—which possessed the Larmenius Charter. Apparently the French Templars had just felt temporarily abandoned by the Scottish strain.

Fabré-Palaprat, who first revealed the Larmenius Charter in 1804, also revealed a Templar document called the *Levitikon*, which was an eleventh century version of the *Gospel of John* with blatantly Gnostic rephrasing. The text consists of two parts, the first describing the nine grades of the Templar Order, which it calls the "Church of John," and explaining that the Templars called themselves "Johannites" or "original Christians." The second part of the *Levitikon* contains the Gospel of John, though it eliminates many of the miracles attributed to Jesus, portraying him more as a man than a god, and portrays Jesus as an initiate of the mysteries of the Egyptian god Osiris. These Egyptian mysteries of Jesus are then said to have been passed on to "John the Beloved," and the text further claims that some of the writings of the disciple Paul show no true knowledge of Jesus' teachings. (Biblical scholars have indeed found that many of the writings of Paul were later forgeries by the early Church, likely by the Bishop Irenaeus, who also published "Against the Heresies" after "new letters of Paul" were conveniently found at the same time.) The Levitikon also records the secret tradition of "Johannite Christians" from the Middle East, and confirms the concept that the word "Christ" was a title that was not reserved only for Jesus, but for all leaders of the Johannite tradition who had attained Gnosis.

Bernard Raymond Fabre- Palaprat was also known for making public his version of the Johannite Church, which led to some divisions within the Templar Order. There were some Templars in France that were hoping to reconcile with the Roman Catholic Church as opposed to supporting the very Gnostic Johannite Church. Ultimately, this led to different strains of the Templar tradition existing with some different philosophical leanings to this day. This will be explored more in a future chapter.

Finally, on consequence of a decree of a Supreme Convention of the Brethren, and by the supreme authority to me committed, I will, declare, and command that the Scottish exemplars, as deserters from the Order, are to be accursed, and that they and the brethren of Saint John of Jerusalem, upon whom may God have mercy, as spoliators of the domains of our soldiery are now and hereafter to be considered as beyond the pale of the Temple I have therefore established signs, unknown to our false Brethren, and not to be known by them, to be orally communicated to our fellow-soldiers, and in which way I have already been pleased to communicate them in the Supreme Convention.

But these signs are only to be made known after due profession and knightly consecrations according to the Statutes, Rites, and Usages of the fellow-soldiery of the Temple, transmitted by me to the above-named Eminent Commander as they there delivered into my hands by the venerable and most holy martyr, our Grand Master, to whom be honor and glory. Let it be done as I have said. So mote it be. Amen.

Above: Words from the Larmenius Charter

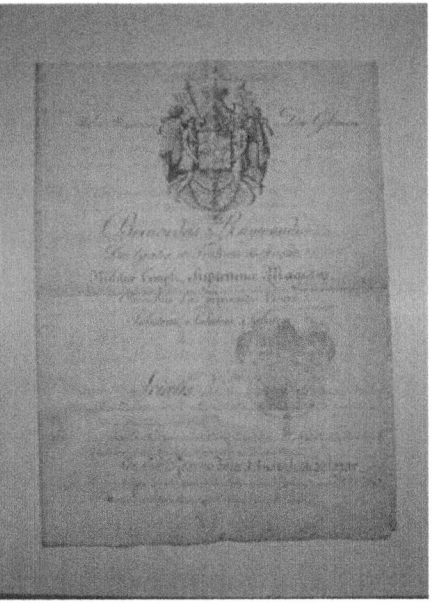

Above Left: Translated Copy of the Larmenius Charter
at Mark Mason Hall in London
Above Right: Initiation certificate of Bernard Raymond Fabre Palaprat

Above: Tau Sendivogius and Tau Emerys in Cords, France, representing two strains of the Templar tradition from Larmenius, with the OST and the OTSI. Photo is taken in a Templar temple in a Cathar cavern, under Bernard Raymond Fabre Palaprat's former home at Cords. (Photo by Paul Dickerson).

IV. The Rose Croix Alchemical Templar Tradition and the Knights of Christ

During the "great escape" of 1307, there were a total of 237 Templars that had escaped from France and took refuge in the Commandery Temple in London, including a Templar alchemist named Guidon de Montanor. Montanor adopted another of the Templar escapees as his spiritual son- a man named Gaston de la Pierre Phoebus, who he taught the alchemical art. After a few months, fearing the greed of King Edward I, these Templars fled to Scotland to the Isle of Mull, and met other Templars there who had traveled by ship. There, Gaston de la Pierre Phoebus created a new group of Templars in a guild of alchemists. Phoebus formed a Templar guild composed of himself, de Montanor, Pierre de Lombardie, Henri de Montfort, Cesar Minvielle, and Pierre-Yorik de Rivault. Their symbol was the pelican pecking its own breast, which had allusions to the sacrifice of Jesus on the one hand, and the fact that during the middle ages, an alchemical vessel was called "a pelican".

Phoebus then later returned discreetly to France with 27 Templars, after persecutions had settled down and Pope Clement V had died, and visited the new Pope John XXII, (who was more sympathetic to the Templar plight). Phoebus taught the pope alchemy in exchange for his blessing to forgive the Order of the past offences, so it could be reinstituted. Pope John XXII agreed to the deal, but in turn then asked Phoebus to return to Scotland and try and persuade his Templar brothers, who were serving with King Robert the Bruce, to return to France, so that some form of reconciliation may take place between the Roman church and Scotland. Phoebus, knowing that the journey back to Scotland could be dangerous, handed over certain documents related to the Templar alchemical secrets at a place called Pont-St. Esprit to a former Templar who had hid within the Knights Hospitallier, and become a Prior of the Hospitalliers of St. John.

On his journey afterward to Scotland, Phoebus and 13 of his Templar brothers were murdered in their travels. However five Templars reached Scotland and later returned to France. They were led by Jasques de Via, who was the nephew of Pope John XXII. Jacques de Via then proceeded to draw up a new Templar Rule, which was adopted by a College of 33 men. The College elected de Via as the successor to Phoebus. On May 6th, 1317, Jacques de Via died, and his successors have since called themselves "Freres Aines de la Rose-Croix", or "Elder Brothers of the Rose Cross", assuming the name which had originally come from the Order that Amus had established centuries before. The tradition continues to this day, and the total number of members of the College remains at 33. Shortly after this episode, Pope John XXII, being true to his word to Phoebus, created a new Papal Bull on March 14th, 1319, which legitimized Templars in Portugal under the new name of the "Knights of Christ", of which there is also much history, especially as related to their sea voyages and ocean conquests, and later association with Columbus. While the Elder Brothers of the Rose Croix continue to exist to this day, the Knights of Christ became a secularized order of merit in 1789, and ceased to operate after the last person (Belgian King Baudouin) was received in it in 1987, and he passed away in July 1993.

V. The Germany and England Affair

The Templar tradition of the Freres Aines de la Rose-Croix are said to have created another division of the Templar Order in Germany called the Militia Crucifera Evangelica, which had its first opening convention on July 27th, 1586, and which likewise used the symbol of the rose cross. The convention was sponsored particularly and specifically by Henry IV, king of France and Navarre, who was also a member of the Ordre des Chevaliers Faydits de la Colombe du Paraclet tradition that Hughes De Payans and Godfrey De Saint Omar had been knighted into. The Militia Crucifera Evangelica installed Frederick, the Duke of Württemberg as its Grand Master in 1598, and Queen Elizabeth I was also a recorded member. The Militia Crucefera Evangelica is first mentioned in publication in Simon Studion's 1598 book entitled the *Naometria*, meaning, the "measurement of the temple". The book is an outline of the allegorical meanings behind King Solomon's Temple, and describe the alchemical, qabbalistic, and Gnostic interpretations behind the allegory of the temple. Out of this Templar current came Johanne Valentine Andreae, who is credited with at least one of the Rosicrucian manifestos of the early 1600s, starting in 1605 and culminating in 1614. (Simon Studion was Andreae's mentor at the Stift in Tubingen). Frederick went on to establish a secret church in Bad Teinacht, Germany, in which secret artifacts and teachings aids were hidden for initiates of the tradition.

Let us here pause, and quickly examine the Rosicrucian manifestos for a moment. The Rosicrucian manifestos claimed that a tomb was found belonging to one "Christian Rosenkreutz," who had lived until the age of 106, and was buried in 1484. This tomb contained all the elements of Rosicrucian philosophy, which included studies related to alchemy, the qabalah, and a true understanding of Christian mysteries. The documents claimed the Rosicrucians were able to heal all of humanity's diseases, bring about spiritual transformation, and transmute base metals into gold (which they considered a talent of lesser importance). The "tomb" of Christian Rosenkreutz was meant as a metaphor for a period of underground activity by the Rosicrucians (who were about to come out into the public view). The anonymous manifestos also spoke out against the abuses of the Roman Catholic Church and the corrupt monarchies of the day. They solicited membership from the intelligentsia of Europe, saying that anyone found worthy to be a member would be contacted. (It was probably assumed that those who published works of philosophical or scientific value and dedicated such works to the Rosicrucians would be considered for membership).

Rumors began to circulate around Europe that the Rosicrucians were actually the Templars, coming into a revival, which were valid, as the whole Templar affair had its roots partially within the Rose Cross Order established by Amus, as discussed previously.

Johanne Valentine Andreae was also in communication and working with Sir Francis Bacon in England, who was also said to be a member of this same movement, and who was said to be the secret child of Queen Elizabeth I herself, and the Earl of Leicester. Legend records how Queen Elizabeth had handed Francis over to Lord Nicolas and Lady Anne Bacon to raise, to ensure that she remained the "Virgin Queen" to maintain control. Francis Bacon was later known to go on and create the *Order of the Helm*, which it has been suggested, was responsible for the writing and production of the Shakespeare plays. By the age of 17, Francis Bacon had been initiated into the Knights Templar in Ambassador Paulets suite in France. Later in life, Bacon composed his unfinished book *The New Atlantis*, in which he writes about a secret society of philosophers that he calls both the "College of Solomon" and the "Brotherhood of Solomon," and which is a society known to use the symbol of the red Templar cross, and who claim to have a knowledge of the entire Earth. The group also possesses the ability to transmute metals, prolong life, and heal injuries through the use of secret elixirs. In Bacon's book, this secret society is said to work behind the scenes in world events, while remaining completely anonymous.

Another example of this connection between the Templar "Rosicrucian" movement between Germany and England can be found on January 6, 1604, when Queen Elizabeth I of England held a masquerade ball at the White Hall. Inigo Jones was asked to design the gentlemen's costumes for the ball. Inigo Jones was a good friend of Francis Bacon, and of Ben Johnson of the Shakespeare folio publications. Jones also designed the Shakespeare play costumes. Why the Queen asked Jones to design the costumes for her ball is not known (though it may well have been at the request of her son Francis Bacon), or because of the same Templar lineage that they all belonged to, related to the Militia Crucifera Evangelica. What is known is that among the sketches of the costumes was one over which Jones wrote the words "A Rosicros." Jones had been drawing since December 1603. Since the ball was to occur on January 6, 1604, and the designs for the costumes had to be distributed several weeks in advance to permit making of the costumes, designs were submitted to the Queen for her approval sometime before Christmas 1603. Furthermore, several other variations of the costume were made for special distinguished guests. Since the title "A Rosicros" was known and used for several costumes in 1603, an organization of that name in England clearly existed by at least 1600, and the Queen was familiar enough with them. This is again, another example of the rose cross appearing as related to the Militia Crucifera Evangelica that Queen Elizabeth I belonged to, and of which Frederick, the Duke of Württemberg was the Grand Master, and which ultimately goes back to the Rose Cross tradition of Amus, aka Arnaud, which was partially at the foundation of the Templar Order.

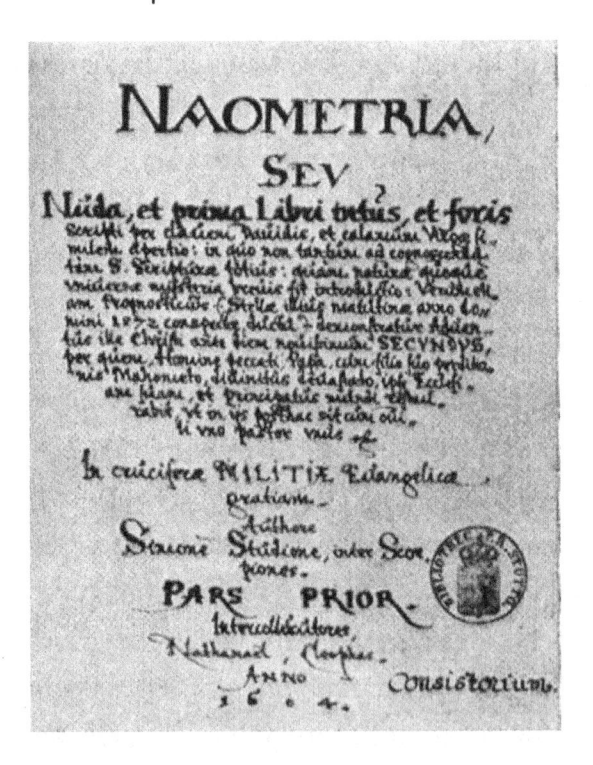

Above: Naometria, written in 1598 and published in 1604. Dedicated to the Militia Crucifera Evangelica. Written by Simone Studion

Above: Frederick, Duke of Wutemberg and his crypt in Tubingen, in which there are red Templar crosses on the walls (below).

Above: Stained glass window in Calw, Germany, of the Andreae family. Notice how the blazon consists of a Saint Andrew's cross surrounded by roses.

Above: Door knob from the 1600s for the secret Templar church, established in Bad Teinacht, by Frederick, the Grand Master of the
Militia Crucefera Evangelica.

Above: The town of Bad Teinacht, with the church that Frederick had established in the background.

Above: Author holding the key to the secret Tracing Board used by the early Rosicrucians of the 1600s, and commissioned by Frederick, which is found in Germany.

Above: Little Hagia Sophia mosque in Istanbul where Hugh De Payans was initiated in 1096, and which later became the Templar Commandery

Above: Templar church in London, which was built in a similar manner to the former Templar Commandery in Constantinople/ Istanbul.

VI. The Society of Unknown Philosophers

Later the Freres Aines de la Rose-Croix also established the Societie des Philosophers Inconnu as early as 1595. Among its leadership is included the alchemist Michael Sendivogius aka Sedziwoj, (who was a teacher of the alchemist Michael Maier in Altdorf and an advisor to Rudolf II in Prague, and who had drawn up the Statutes of the Society). Another member of the Society was the alchemist Thomas Vaughan (aka Eugenius Philalethes- meaning: Eirenaios "peaceful", Philos "friend", Aletheia "truth"). Thomas Vaughan was known to have been an advisor to many of the people who formed the Royal Society of Britain, to include early Masons like Robert Moray, Elias Ashmole, and Jean Theophilus Desaguliers. In fact, tradition has stated that the Society of Unknown Philosophers acted incognito under the name of the "Cabala Club", which many of the members who founded the Masonic Grand Lodge of England in 1717 belonged to. A Dr. John Byrom ran the "Cabala Club", which met on the same evenings and in the same location as The Globe Lodge No. 23 - the members of both groups being the same. The Cabala Club was attended by people like Desaguliers, Stuckeley, and Sloane, who were all prominent Freemasons who helped to draft and create the systems of Freemasonry that developed in the 1700s under the newly formed Grand Lodge of England.

This same Society of Unknown Philosophers was said to give birth to the tradition known as "Martinism" under the direction of Louis Claude de Saint Martin, in the late 1700s, which has an "Unknown Superior" Degree, and which refers to Louis Claude de Saint Martin as the "Unknown Philosopher". Likewise, it was said to have originally had close relations to the Rectified Scottish Rite system of Freemasonry under John Baptiste Willermoz, who was close friends with Louis Claude du Saint Martin. Both of these two individuals had been initiated by Martinez de Pasqually, who was himself of the Unknown Philosopher Templar tradition. Martinez de Pasqually created his own degree system, which included a Chevalier of the Temple degree. This is why his student John Baptist Willermoz created the Rectified Scottish Rite, which also has Templar ceremonies of the Ordre de Chevalier Bienfaisant de la Cité Sainte'. Around the same time, Baron von Hund created his Strict Templar Observance Freemasonry after orders from an "Unknown Superior".

According to the Strict (Templar) Observance tradition, it is stated that on October 16th, 1311, at the Council of Vienna, the Templar Order was not only declared finished, but 54 Templars were killed in Paris in a single day. The tradition goes on to say that Templars fled to northern lands, in particular Sweden, Norway, Ireland and Scotland. A certain Peter Aumont, who was Provincial Master of Auvergne, along with two other Commanders and five knights, changed their names and disguised themselves as stone masons. Aumont called himself Mabeignac from that point forward, and arrived in Ireland in the year 1311. From Ireland, they then fled to Scotland, to the Island of Mull. Here they met George Harris, who was Grand Commander of Hampton Court. Together they agreed to protect the Templar Order underground, and started a secret Templar tradition on Saint John the Baptist Day of 1312. Aumont then passed away of old age in the year 1313, and Harris was elected to replace his leadership. Under Harris, it is said that all knights were permitted again to marry in order to preserve and perpetuate the Order, and for 250 years, you had to be the son of one of these Templars to be admitted into the tradition. Harris was said to have established the seal of his lineage as a phoenix with the words Perit, ut vivat- or, "he dies that he may live." This Order was said to eventually become The Rite of Strict Observance Freemasonry.

I may quickly add that the Order of the Temple of Secret Initiates Templar lineage claims as one of its past Grand Masters Joséphin Aïme Péladan (1859-1918), who had been introduced to the Order by his brother Dr. Adrien Péladan (1844-1885). Josephin Péladan had likewise been on the Martinist Supreme Council under Papus, and he initiated Emile Dantinne (1883-1969), (also known as Sar Heironimous), who helped start the FUDOSI, and was known for his Rosicrucian work in Toulouse. Dr. Adrien Péladan had likewise belonged to a Templar alchemical lineage going back to Cagliostro and the Comte de Saint Germaine.

The esoteric author and historian Manly Palmer Hall makes mention of the Society of Unknown Philosophers in his work *Rosicrucian and Masonic Origins*, thus:
"Long before the establishment of Freemasonry as a fraternity, a group of mystics founded in Europe what was called the "Society of Unknown Philosophers." Prominent among the profound thinkers who formed the membership of this society were the alchemists, who were engaged in transmuting the political and religious "base metal" of Europe into ethical and spiritual "gold"; the Qabbalists who, as investigators of the superior orders of Nature, sought to discover a stable foundation for human government; and lastly the astrologers who, from a study of the procession of the heavenly bodies, hoped to find therein the rational archetype for all mundane procedure."

Above Left: Templar flag, the "Beauceant".   Above Right: Martinist pantical.

SOMMAIRE ABREGE[1]
De tout ce qui est contenu dans ces Lettres, renfermé dans un Sceau ou Hieroglife de la Société des Philosophes inconnus.

C E caractère n'a pas été inventé & choisi au hazard & sans dessein : Car le Trident est le Neptune de nous

The hieroglyphic seal of the Society of Unknown Philosophers.
(The version from the printed edition.)

Above: Symbol for the Unknown Philosophers, which was a trident. The trident was a particular symbol used by the Grand Master of the Templar Order, and is still used to this day. From the trident is also derived the symbol of the fleur-de-lis. Within Martinist traditions to this day, the three branched candelabra is likewise used whenever the Grand Master is present, which looks similar to this the central part of this symbol.

VII. Holy Saints John and the Johannite Gnostic Tradition

The subject of the Holy Saints John has been written about so many times by Masonic authors, since they are mentioned in the current Masonic degrees around the world. In Freemasonry, in particular, John the Baptist and John the Evangelist are emphasized as "two early patrons of Freemasonry". There is an important perspective regarding them that has been almost totally lost among most Masonic researchers however, which deserves our consideration. This involves the exploration of them from the Gnostic perspective, which never viewed the John's of the Bible as merely just personalities that played a side role to Jesus, but rather a tradition unto themselves that even represented an aspect of the Grand Architect of the Universe. Accordingly, the Templar tradition has had an undercurrent of Johannite Gnosticism attached to it since the foundation of the Templar Order, as explained in previous chapters.

We will not recap here the general interpretations of the Holy Saints John that Masonic authors regularly recap, regarding things like how the saint days of John the Baptist and John the Evangelist correspond to the Solstices and other such ideas of which the Gnostics were intimately aware, but rather we will view the subject from a fresh perspective that has been secretly preserved by Templars of all ages, and which has escaped the persecuting hands of orthodoxy in ages past. I will also not explore a more general explanation of Gnosticism and it's connection with Freemasonry, which I have done in other publications, and which has been explored by other authors. In general, however, let it be known that the goal of the Gnostics was to attain the Light of Gnosis, or divine revelatory knowledge, which led to Mastery and salvation, and that this Gnosis usually came after a series of initiatic purifications that prepared the initiate for this awakening after a symbolic death and raising and the communication of secret password, grips, and signs of the hands and feet. There were many Gnostic traditions, under names like Valentinians, Manichians, Sophians, Paulicans, Tawhid Druze, Sufi, and others, which more or less shared similar ideas and doctrines, and many of which referred to themselves as the "Sons of Light"- just as Masons do today.

Let us begin our subject of this chapter by quoting Eliphas Levi, the eccentric Roman Catholic Priest, of whom Albert Pike copies so much from in *Morals and Dogma*, and who was known to be a member of the Martinist current. The following is from a personal letter he wrote to a Mr. Montaunt, who revealed it in turn to Lucien Mauchel, who later gave it to the Martinist periodical *L'Intiation* in 1891. The critical and informed reader will immediately begin to notice a similar passage that Pike borrowed from Eliphas Levi for *Morals and Dogma*: "The official Church, which declares itself infallible in the interpretation of the Scriptures, never could explain the Apocalypse, which is the kabbalistic key of the Gospels, and there always has been in Christianity an Occult or Johannite Church, which while respecting the need for the official Church, preserved from dogma an interpretation quite other than that which is given to the profane. The Templars, the Rosicrucians, the Freemasons of high rank have, all before the French Revolution, belonged to this church of which Martinez de Pasqalis, Louis Claude de Saint Martin, and even Mme de Krudemer have been the apostles in the last century (1800s). The distinctive character of this school is to avoid publicity and never constitute itself into a dissident sect. The Count Joseph de Maistre, thus so catholic, was, more than one might believe, sympathetic to the Martinist Society and announced a coming regeneration of the dogma by lights, which would emanate from sanctuaries of occultism. There are still now enthusiastic priests who are Initiates of the ancient doctrines, and a bishop, inter alia, recently dead, who had requested of me kabbalistic communications. The disciples of Saint-Martin call themselves Unknown Philosophers and those of a modern Master, happy enough to be even more ignored, have no need to assume any name, for the world does not even suspect their existence."

So what of this secret Johannite Tradition? Some researchers have written on a Gnostic group known as the Mandeans of the Middle East, who are known for their veneration of John the Baptist, and who have been called by explorers as early as Marco Polo as "John Christians". In fact, not only do they venerate John the Baptist, but there is some indication they view him as a Prophet even greater than Jesus. This may come from the New Testament passage where Jesus says that of man born of woman, none is greater than John the Baptist. This group, which largely is in charge of the gold trade in places like Iraq, have been and continue to be persecuted. Many associate them with Sabbeans, which is a tradition that is believed to have come out of the southern region of what is now modern Turkey, and was formerly called Harran, and who are mentioned as *People of the Book* in the Qur'an, (along with Jews, Christians and Muslims). The Sabbeans were known for venerating Idris of the Quran, (Enoch of the Bible), who they associated with Hermes of the Hermetic tradition, and much of their doctrines seem to be of Egyptian and Hermetic origin. There may even be some connection with another group known by a similar name, which is the "Sabians", which come from Ethiopia and are believed to be of Solomon's wife, the Queen of Sheba's early city. "Sheba" became "Saba", and so they were known as "Sabians". Over time however, the Mandeans have taken many of the attributes of Hermes and attributed them to John the Baptist, and have emulated his baptisms in initiation rites involving secret signs of the hands and feet, and secret passwords that are communicated at initiation ceremonies. Many of these secret grips and signs find resonance in Templar, Rosicrucian and Masonic degree work, though many of the same attributes have been passed on by the Sufi and the Tawhid Druze Gnostic traditions in places like Egypt, Turkey, Syria, and Lebanon. Being Gnostic traditions, which interpret scripture symbolically and personally, it is not surprising that all these groups are regularly persecuted by more fundamentalist religious persuasions in the areas they reside. As mentioned previously, all of these groups were, according to historical record, associated with by the Templars. The name "Mandeans" comes from the word "Manada", which means "Gnosis".

Before we fall into the mistake of believing that a Johannite Tradition can only be found in areas of the Middle East with groups like the Mandeans however, it is worthy to note that a tradition preserving a secret Johannite text experienced significant persecution in Europe during one of the earliest Crusades, which took place in southern France! The group being persecuted was the Albigensiens, or Cathars, which we have discussed with the formation of the Templars. One reason they were thought to be persecuted is that they valued a secret Bogomil book above all others called Interrogatio Johannis (The Questions of John), or the full title of "Interrogatio Iohannis apostoli et evangelistae in cena secreta regni coelorum de ordinatione mundi istius et de principe et de Adam." It was also available in different forms under the name of the *Secret Supper Book of John the Evangelist* and *The Book of John the Evangelist*. There are two surviving versions of the text: one was discovered in the archives of the Inquisition kept at the French town of Carcassonne in Languedoc, and the other is found in the National Library of Vienna. There are some differences in both texts, suggesting that they both come from an earlier original that has not survived.

It is worthy to re-mention that many of the original Knights Templar came from Cathar families, and Saint Bernard, who had written the Rule of the Templars, had praised the Cathars calling them more Christian than the Christians in Rome! However they suffered a terrible fate at the hands of Inquisition and a Roman Catholic Army led by Simon de Montfort, that probably wanted to seize land in the Languedoc region of France, and consequently murdered hundreds of thousands of Cathars beginning in 1147, developing more widespread in 1208, and finally ending in 1321. It is known that Templars gave safe shelter to Cathar families, and Lord Raymond VI, who was the Cathar defender, was later denied burial on Holy Land, and so he was buried in the Templar Commandery in Toulouse.

What was it about this secret book of John that was considered so heretical by the Roman Catholic Church? The book is a question and answer dialogue between John the Evangelist and God, in which John *represents an aspect of God* talking to Himself, and in which it is described how Satan, and not God, created this world, and how various Prophets and Saints, and even Jesus, were sent to try to wake people up out of their imprisoned slumber. It emphasizes how God has tried to intervene in changing the creation that Satan had made. It also mentions how John the Baptist was the reincarnation of the prophet Elijah, and how he preserved the initiations to purify men back to the light of Gnosis (divine revelatory knowledge), which brought about salvation. However, it also says that the Gnosis and the salvation can only come by also doing good works, and that even if someone is baptized, if they do not the "work of God", then they will not be saved. The text also speaks of the Apocalypse, traditionally associated with another John, that of Patmos, as mentioned in the New Testament *Revelations*. Other Gnostic traditions who have been called Johannite, have interpreted *Revelations* as related to the dying of the old self, and the awakening of the True Self to Gnosis, and that there are many Gnostic, Gematria, and Qabbalistic elements to the narrative that gets completely lost on the uninitiated.

It is significant that the Cathar text is associated with the three John's of the Bible, and later Gnostic movements in Europe associated with Johannism likewise venerated all Johns of the Bible as aspects of one Archetypal aspect of God. The Cathars were also known to have an idol, which was deemed to be the perfect embodiment of man, called the "Perfecti", which some scholars have associated with John, though others think it may have also represented Pythagoras. This same term, *Perfecti*, was applied to one of the higher degrees of the Cathar stages of initiation, and which represented Mastery from Gnosis, and that one had become a Son or Daughter of Light, and had achieved a level of perfection in which one did not have to reincarnate anymore. The Perfecti were known to wear white robes- similar to the Highest grade of the Druids, and the dress of the Templar tunics.

Above: Cathar "Perfecti" idol

There is a belief that one of the mysteries associated with this name of "John", is that it is derived from the Greek "Ioannes". This name was deemed significant because of the emphasis on the Greek vowels of I-O-A. These vowels were considered by many Gnostic traditions to be the secret name of God. The letter "I" represented the Logos, or Word of God, as well as a point becoming a line; the letter "O" represented the Christos, or realized consciousness of God, as well as a line reconnecting to itself after its extension in the curved Universe, and therefore a circle; and the letter "A" represented the "Sophia", or reflection of God in matter, as well as the triangle that forms when two extremes come in contact to form a third point. Sometimes the "A" was represented by some Gnostic traditions as a set of compasses, which can extend itself to manifest the circle, or the consciousness of God. As such, the sacred name IOA was also sometimes depicted as IAO. Either way, it was at the root of the Greek name for John.

The Gnostics also observed and suggested that consonants represented physical forms and vowels represented the spirit behind the physical forms. They stated that the main vowels could be broken down, or reduced, to the vowels IAO, as "I" could also be pronounced "eee", or "E", and "A" could also be pronounced "ahhh", and "O" could also be pronounced "ooo" or "U". The Freemason would do well to observe that the only vowels in the first two degree passwords are OA and AI. This emphasis is also found in words like "A-dO-naI" and "JI-hO-vAh".

As late as the 1803 there was a new Gnostic Church manifestation started by French Templars called the Johannite Church of Primitive Christians, under the leadership of Templar Grand Master Bernard-Raymond Fabre-Palaprat, (who was also a prominent Freemason in France). This church later had close ties with Martinist movements, which developed into l'Englise Catholique Gnostique under the influence of Gerard Encausse (Papus), and which ultimately had influence on the creation of later Gnostic churches like the Ecclesia Gnostica of California, under the direction of Bishop Stephan Hoeller, and the Gnostic Sanctuary of California under Bishop Rosamonde Miller, as well as other traditions. The Johannite Church itself continues to exist today in different countries around the world, and in particular under the name of the Apostolic Johannite Church, or AJC. The leaders of the Johannite Church have always assumed the title of "Joahnnes", or "John", and have formed a successive line of "Holy Saints John". They have maintained close ties with the Order of the Temple of Secret Initiates, a Knight Templar lineage, which works in leadership capacity for a pre-study Order known as the Templar Collegia, of which its membership is composed of many people of Masonic and Rosicrucian backgrounds, as well as Druze, Sufi, Druid, First Nation Native Indigenous American, Tibetan, and others. These Gnostic church traditions continue to regularly celebrate Templars and the Templar tradition in their mass, and in particular during the "Litany" of Pontiffs of the traditions, and during the "Consecration".

It is also worth mentioning, that in the Grail legend of *Parzival*, by Wolfram von Eschenbach, (which was published in the first quarter of the 13th century), and has a story in which Templars are the Grail Guardians, and which the Grail King's brother marries the Grail Maiden and has a lineage of new Grail Kings. In *Parzival*, it is said that the name of the Grail Kings ever after was "John", and that this is the origin of the famous "Prester John", of which the early medieval world was obsessed, and of whom Marco Polo sought to find. The book *Parzival* says:

"Only now could Repanse de Schoye (the Grail Maiden, whose name means the "response that is chosen") be glad of her journey. Later in India she bore a son named 'John'. They called him 'Prester John', and, ever since, they call all their kings by no other name…"

In this text from the middle ages, we find a story connecting both the Templars, and a tradition associated with a lineage of John's, much like we find with the current Templar movement and the Apostolic Johannite Church tradition.

The story of the Johannite Tradition goes much further than the scope of this article, but needless to say, the tradition has claimed such notables as Leonardo Da Vinci and others. From a Johannite perspective, then, the two Saints John in Freemasonry represents something much more than two early patrons of Freemasonry. Rather, they represent a lineage of Johns who have passed on the secret Gnostic Tradition, and wherever the name "John" shows up, it is usually an allusion to this tradition, which was inherited by the early Templars and passed on to Freemasonry. Take for example, the herb Saint John's Wort, which was named by early American alchemists who were believed to be passing on this tradition. Or take the American term "Yankee", which comes from the Dutch name for "John"- which is "Yan", and where a bunch of "Johns" would be "Yankees". There are countless other examples, with the point that "John" alluded to much more than just a saint- or two saints, or even a fleeting Christian reference in Freemasonry. Masonic catechisms will emphasize that the Mason has come from a lodge of the "Holy Saints John of Jerusalem".

Any student of Roman Catholic saints knows that the patron saint of Masonry is Saint Stephen- who is not even mentioned in Freemasonry. Saint Stephen is also the patron saint of Deacons- which is about a close a connection to Freemasonry as you can get, since Freemasonry has two Deacon positions in most jurisdictions, though they serve more of a server role than a religious one. We are left to wonder then, why John the Baptist and John the Evangelist are emphasized in Freemasonry in place of Saint Stephen? It is the view of this author, as well as many others throughout history, that part of its emphasis in Freemasonry is due to its Gnostic and Templar heritage, of which ritual compilers like Desagulier in the early 1700s were very aware of. Let us not forget that it was on Saint John the Baptist day, of 1717, that the Grand Lodge of England announced itself. This emphasis of John the Baptist has likewise had its place not only among the Gnostics, but also among the alchemists (many of whom named themselves after famous Gnostic leaders of the past), and in the Grail Legends themselves.

In conclusion, there has been a Gnostic tradition associated with the very name of John, and Pike was correct in emphasizing it in *Morals and Dogma*. Even though he perpetuated the idea by pulling from Eliphas Levi, even Levi himself was aware of the tradition and knew that it was a great secret among Templars, high degree Freemasons, Martinists, and others. This same "John" emphasis is found across a wide spectrum of the Western esoteric traditions, and many Orders, which continue to have this emphasis. Many of these traditions have a Templar foundation. The Johannism that is found in Freemasonry, is one more landmark of its former connection with the Templars in a distant age. It certainly opens up the symbolism of the Saints John to further speculation, by those who dare to know!

Above: Apostolic Johannite Church clergy, including Patriarch Sovereign Pontiff, Tau Ioanness IV, and Bishop Mar Thomas, along with author (serving as OTSI Grand Master).

Left: Bishop Rosamonde Miller of the Gnostic Sanctuary with a Templar cross.
Right: Bishop Stephan Hoeller of the Ecclesia Gnostica with Templar flag.

VIII. Melchizadek, the Christos, the Paraclete, and the Grail

Fundamental to the Templar tradition has been found the idea of Melchizadek. The name "Melchizadek" is said to come from the Hebrew "Melki" meaning "King/Teacher", and "Tzaddiq" meaning "righteousness". Others have suggested that the origin of the name can actually be found in the Phoenician Meilki-Sydyk, where "Meilki" means "Lord", and "Sydyk" was the god of justice and was an attribute of El- the Most High God in the Phoenician pantheon. The following are references to Melchizadek in the Bible:

And Melchizadek King of Salem brought forth bread and wine; and he was the priest of the most high God.

And he blessed him, and said, Blessed be Abram of the most High God possessor of heaven and earth.

And blessed be the most high God, which hath delivered thine enemies into thy hand. And he gave him tithes of all.
(Genesis 14, 18-20)

The Lord hath sworn, and will not repent, Thou art a priest forever after the order of Melchizadek.
(Psalms 110, 4)

For this Melchizadek, King of Salem, priest of the most high God, who met Abraham returning from the slaughter of the kings, and blessed him;
To whom also Abraham gave a tenth part of all; first being by

interpretation King of righteousness, and after that also King of Salem, which is, King of peace;
Without father, without mother, without descent, having neither beginning of days, nor end of life; but made like unto the son of God; abideth a priest forever.
Now consider how great he was, unto whom even the patriarch Abraham gave the tenth of the spoils.
And it is yet far more evident; for that after the similitude of Melchizadek there arises another priest,
Who is made, not after the law of carnal commandment, but after the power of endless life.
For those priests were made without oath, but this with an oath by him that said unto him, The Lord sware and will not repent, Thou are a priest forever after the order of Melchizadek.
(Hebrews 7, 1-21)

According to Templar tradition, this episode in the Bible is describing the first initiation, in which Abram is initiated into a state of peace, after which he is given bread and wine- products of human industry and creativity. After this initiation, he changes his name to Abraham. Abraham had conquered the warring elements in himself and therefore came to peace. Abraham later went on to have two sons- Isaac and Ishmael, whose blood lines in turn led to the religions of Christianity and Islam.

In the Biblical passages related to Melchizadek, it says he blessed from the "Most High God", which is El in Hebrew, and which has its root in the Phoenician "El-Elyon", representing the first Light of Creation, and the Universal God. In Egypt, this concept was represented by the Aton, from which the Hebrew word "Adonai" is also derived. The place that Melchizadek established was

Jerusalem, coming from the Phoenician "Ur-Shalim", meaning "the spirit of Shalim"- or "the place of peace". "Shalim" was also said to be the son of El within the Phoenician pantheon tradition, who was the god of dusk, or the time of rest from the day's labors, and consequently related to the Hebrew word "Shalom"- meaning "peace".

Biblical passages also describe Melchizadek as "without father, without mother, without descent, having neither beginning of days nor end of life..." Here we need to ask ourselves, what has no father, no mother, no lineal descent, and without beginning or end? The answer to this riddle is *consciousness*. We are not talking about the consciousness that is said to come from the brain, but rather the Universal Consciousness that is said to give birth to everything- including the consciousness associated with the brain. Consciousness is said to be the son, or product, of the Universal Light, the Most High God- El-Elyon, and hence why it is the "son of God" and abides as a priest forever. Consciousness is what initiates us into the state of profound peace, when we can reconcile the warring elements within ourselves.

In the Templar tradition, the "bread" and "wine" that Melchizadek serves relate to alchemical substances that were likewise called "manna" and "blood of Christ" in the Bible. Herein is the mystery why even in the Dead Sea Scrolls, there are descriptions of the "Teacher of Righteousness", which is something to be ingested. Templar alchemists have asserted that anytime the Bible refers to bread, manna, shu-bread, salt, or white stone, that it is alluding to the alchemical substance known as "manna". Hidden in this mystery are the keys to the Holy Grail- which was so venerated by Templars. In fact, in Wolfram von

Eschenbach's *Parzival*, he recounts how the Templars guard the Holy Grail, in which the phoenix is mentioned, as it relates to alchemy, and something from the Phoenician and Egyptian traditions. Wolfram von Eschenbach says:

"[The Grail] is well known to me…many formidable fighting men dwell at Munsalvaesche (the mountain of salvation) with the Grail. They are continually riding out on sorties in quest of adventure. Whether these same Templars reap trouble or renown, they bear it for their sins. A warlike company lives there. I will tell you how they are nourished. They live from a Stone whose essence is most pure. If you have never heard of it I shall name it for you here. It is called "Lapsit exilis." By virtue of this Stone the Phoenix is burned to ashes, in which he is reborn. Thus does the Phoenix moult its feathers! Which done, it shines dazzling bright and lovely as before! Further: however ill a mortal may be, from the day on which he sees the Stone he cannot die for that week, nor does he lose his colour. For if anyone, maid or man, were to look at the Grail for two hundred years, you would have to admit that his colour was as fresh as in his early prime, except that his hair would grey! Such powers does the Stone confer on mortal men that their flesh and bones are made young again. This Stone is also called "The Grail."

In Templar alchemy, this stone can only be produced from a product of visualization, and uniting one's consciousness with the Universal Consciousness, and ultimately the use of it is the result of health of the body and the elevation of consciousness itself. In other words, one *becomes* the embodiment of Melchizadek- or consciousness. The Philosopher's Stone is the Grail, and it is the physical manifestation of the internal mastery of consciousness.

Templar tradition has also maintained that the Christos is not the last name of Jesus as some seem to think! Rather, it is the *experience* of the universal consciousness as it manifests in the individual and in the world. This is why Jesus performs the communion ritual in the manner of Melchizadek, and why he is forever "of the order of Melchizadek"- as the Christos (or the experience of Universal Consciousness) is a product of Melchizadek, or consciousness itself. Christos means "anointed one", which is the feeling that one has when universal consciousness manifests. To the Templar then, the "second coming of Christ" is not a story about a future embodiment of the man god Jesus coming back to the world to solve the world's problems, but rather it has to do with the manifestation and realization of the Universal consciousness in each individual- *by their own effort*! The first coming of Christ is the realization of it's potential- which comes from the reading of the story of the exemplar Jesus. The second coming then happens *when we embody the Christos ourselves*. As the Christ said, "verily I say unto you, these miracles you see me perform, ye shall do also...and those even greater than these."(John 14:12).

We would do well to also point out that Jesus was said to be born in Bethlehem, which means "house of bread", and is born from Maria, meaning "sea"- which is what salt comes from when the salt water is heated. The sea water gives a virgin birth to salt. Further, salt crystalizes in the shape of a cube, and when a cube is unfolded, you get a cross. Herein is found alchemical metaphors once again. From the alchemical salt is born the alchemical "blood of Christ"...the white cube bleeds.

Furthermore, Jesus is a Nazorean- coming from the Aramaic root "Nazor", which means "forehead". It is within the forehead that the consciousness manifests. Some have related this to the "third eye" in mystical tradition, or the psychic organ of perception and visualization into the true nature of things, also called the anja chakra in eastern traditions. Further, he later attains "anastasis", which means "awakening" (though it is usually translated as "resurrection"), after he is crucified at Golgotha- a word meaning "skull"- or in other words, in his head. Each person must come to recognize the limitations of their physical existence and die to attachment to it, before they can come to realize or awake to their connection with the Universal Consciousness of the Creator. In other words, they must leave the attachment to the physical cave (the skull), and expand their consciousness beyond the body and physical things.

This brings us to the Paraclete. Jesus says that one will come after him that is known as the Paraclete (John 14:16). The word has come to mean "comforter", and Christian theologians have interpreted it as another name for the Holy Spirit. Muslim sheiks have interpreted the Paracete as a reference to Mohammed, or even a reference to the future Mehdi, (who is meant to be the next great Master to come after Jesus). The Templar will recognize that both are correct, though not in the way that they may be presenting it. As Louis Claude de Saint Martin says, "the great misfortune of man is not that he is unaware of truth, but that he misconstrues its nature."

The mystery of the Paraclete has to do with the responsibility that arises when one has connected with the greater consciousness of creation. If we follow the steps outlined above, then Melchizadek represents the Universal consciousness, and the Christ represents the realization of the Universal consciousness, and thereby the Paraclete is the understanding of seeing the bigger picture and acting accordingly after such realization. This is what makes the Paraclete the "comforter", or the one who provides comfort after being struct by compassion while seeing the bigger order to things.

So it is, that the Paraclete is the act of responsible living in attunement with the Universal Consciousness of the All after one has realized the Christos. In this way, anyone acting as the Paraclete *is a comforter*, and is acting from a sacred and holy spirit. *They will be acting as the saviors of the world*. It is not one person per se, any more than Christ is one person, *but rather it is the potential within all people*.

In this way, the mysteries of Melchizadek, the Christos, and the Paraclete, are the mysteries of the Holy Grail... If we were to only mention one other archetypal figure, it would be the Sophia, *which represents the wisdom of the world on how best to act, and is a symbol of the soul personality of each so- called "individual"*. In Templar tradition, Mary Magdalene represented the Sophia, and Jesus represented the Christos, and their union represented the soul coming to the experience of the full consciousness of God. In this sense, their union brings about, or gives birth to, the Paraclete. It creates the enthroned Sophia, as the individual soul returns to the One that unites all conscious beings. These are fundamental aspects of the Templar tradition, and by extension the Gnostic and alchemical traditions that have come out of this tradition. They are also mysteries that take place *in ourselves*.

The mystery of the Jesus and Mary Magdalene has less to do with a physical marriage, union, and blood line (as some would suggest). Rather, it is about a deeper Gnostic mystery, even though there have been some blood lines who have perpetuated this mystery along their family lines from generation to generation.

These are the reasons why in the Grail legends, the "Grail Maiden" (Sophia), handles the Grail cup or "receptacle" (representative of the tradition of Melchizadek), in which the blood of the Christos resides, and a Holy Dove (symbol of the Holy Spirit and the Paraclete) comes down to it. The soul is united with the elements of its Universal nature and consciousness, and in this mystery, all Gnosis is realized and manifested. Through this act, the waste land can be healed, as the connection between what is in us and what is out of us is reconciled.

Melchizadek is the foundation however, and it is for this reason that Melchizadek is venerated, and it is the origin as to why most Christian priests of the different denominations are installed after the "order of Melchizadek".

It has been suggested that these stages of human consciousness can also be represented by the development and awakening of humanity's consciousness as a whole. Consequently, the Age of Melchizadek occurred with the tribal traditions of social organization that was generally represented by the Torah or Old Testament times. The Age of awakening to the Christos has been over the last 2,000 years and started with the work of the exemplar Jesus, and has included newer levels of revelation which include movements like Islam, and with it, it's Hermetic and Gnostic undertones. We are now, at the dawn of Aquarius, the vessel carrier, and we are going into the Age of the Paraclete. Each person must become the embodiment of the Christos, and by extension, become the Paraclete. This will bring about the more balanced and compassionate perspective that is needed to heal the wasteland of the world, and consequently the Grail will be made manifest.

There is more to this mystery, but suffice to say, this is enough for any reader to meditate on at this time. If understood, then it is perhaps enough for all time, as within it is contained all wisdom, all mastery, and all reintegration with the Source. Partaking of the Grail is the experience of Gnosis. We are all the Grail Quester Parzival, and we are all the Grail King that needs to be healed.

Above: Melchizadek at Chartres Cathedral

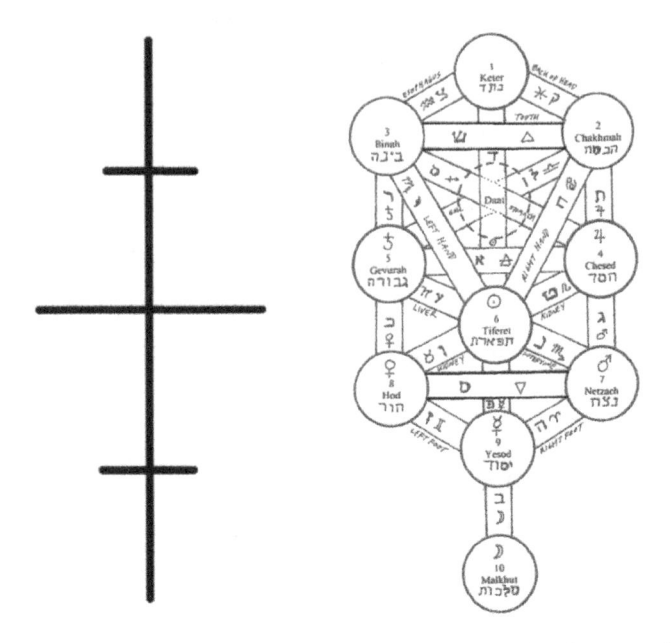

Above Left: Cross of Loraine- a symbol traditionally used by the Grand Master and Grand Commanders of the Templar Order, and representing the three stages of ascending consciousness. It is derived from the qabbalistic tree of life and its middle pillar and three horizontal steps (above right).

Above: author opening the tomb of Rabbi Shimon Bar Yochai, who is widely believed to have co-authored the Zohar. Photo by Paul Dickerson.

IX. Living As an Expression of Templar Spiritual Chivalry

It becomes the responsibility of Templars in the Third Millennium to practice "spiritual chivalry", for spiritual chivalry is the way of the Templar. What is meant by this? Chivalry, of course, is the moral code of ethics from the Middle Ages, in which one sacrifices self for other. It goes without saying, that this should be enough. However people love to discriminate and say to themselves, I will go out of my way for such and such person because they are the same religious persuasion as myself, (or sect, or race, or economic class, or gender, or any number of other distinctions of separateness). By saying "spiritual chivalry", it is implying that we are being chivalrous, *but because of our spiritual Source- which is the same as everyone else's spiritual Source*. Therefore we are chivalrous towards all- regardless of their religious background or persuasion, and regardless of other ways of discriminating and separating ourselves from the One Source. *The same sacred flame is in everyone*!

Practicing spiritual chivalry is very much like the eastern saying "Namaste", meaning, the divine in me celebrates (or recognizes) the divine in you. We do what is good and right not because we are following a strict moral code or oath, but because our true inner nature, the sacred flame within, mandates that we do what is good and right for the developing consciousness of everyone involved- at any moment and in any situation. Thinking and acting in this way requires a great deal more Mastery. You must think before you act or react at all times, and allow for a moment of attunement to the situation and the impulses of the conscience in the heart. At first this can feel like you are taking a long time to respond, but with practice it will come more instantly.

This brings us to the Templar motto: *Non nobis Domine, non nobis, sed nomine tuo da gloriam*. In other words, "not to us, oh Lord, not to us, but to Thy name be the glory!" To understand and act according to this dictate means to be able to completely surrender the personal ego/lower survival based nature to the higher nature and promptings of the soul. In other words, the soul (knight) can direct the horse (ego) towards the Holy Land, and not allow the horse to run rampant in any direction it wants. This necessitates that action arises not for the satisfaction of feeling "superior", but rather it arises due to a natural resonance with the greater order of things, developing into greater degrees of *self-awareness*. By acting in this way, the Chevalier Templar is doing things not because his personal will imposes it, but because he is submitting to a higher will of God, in realization of the natural order of consciousness that is unfolding.

The nine original Templar knights renounced all of their possessions to become the "Poor of Christ", and took three vows on June 12th, 1118, during a ceremony at the Castle of Arginy, in what today is the County of Rhone. In so doing, they voluntarily assumed the following three vows: 1) the vow of chastity, 2) the vow of poverty, and 3) the vow of obedience. Each of these three vows have a precise influence on the psyche of the individual. The vow of Chastity requires that the energy of sexuality be sublimated to create forms other than physical bodies, and results in dominion over the demands of the body. This is the beginning of mastering what is called the "kundalini energy" in the body. The second vow of Poverty requires that the energy which feeds the ego-needs of the personality be sublimated in the service of the soul's higher nature, or the soul's divinity. This results in dominion over the seductive demands of social pride. While the vow of Obedience requires that the personality sublimates its preferences to become available to another voice...for until it can silence its own chattering of the ego, it will never hear the impulses of intuition, nor that of the spiritual archetype which links the soul with its divine source- the Christos. It results in dominion over the demands of the ego image.

This does not mean that the Templar of our modern age needs to give everything up, as the Templars in the past did. These elements should be regularly considered in the daily life of every Templar however, and each Templar should constantly be evaluating where their attachment is to the things that these vows are designed to shake us loose from. The end goal of these three vows are just as relevant today, as they were 900 years ago.

The Templar of today has the same mission as the Templar from 900 years ago, in that as Templars we are to seek out, preserve, protect, and integrate the sacred teachings from the Primordial Tradition, wherever they may manifest. The Templar is not concerned with falling into feelings of spiritual sectarianism, but rather understands that the sacred can be found within. Therefore the Templar is comfortable worshiping in any religious institution, and any place of pure spiritual expression. The Templar is not critical of the manifestation, but is attuned to the Source. The Templar is as comfortable worshipping in the church as he is in the mosque, or the synagogue, or even in a sacred grove of oak trees... Wherever the Templar goes, God is. Consequently, the Templar seeks out, and works with, the leaders of the different spiritual and religious persuasions, in order to be an ambassador for the things of the spirit, and to help bring people back together in common love of their common Source.

The Templar is confident in their actions, because they are rooted in, and should be expressions of, the Grand Architect's infinite love and compassion for creation itself. Therefore the Templar has fought the warring elements within himself or herself, and now is an expression of the internal peace.

Those who have really found this inner peace, and this inner certainty, have assumed the designation of being part of what has been called the "Great White Brotherhood", the "Unknown Superiors", the "Unknown Philosophers", and the "Invisible College", (according to different traditions that have come out of the Templar tradition). Regardless of their culture, or race, or socio-economic background, they form a truly Universal Religion, whose only doctrines come from within. To quote past Grand Commander and Regent to the Grand Master position, Dr. Onslow Wilson, from his book *Psyche's Secret: The Path of Personal Integration*:

"The Universal practice of such a religion is the ultimate goal of all genuine mystery schools, be they in the form of religious denomination, or a school of philosophy and chivalry. The individual practitioners of this universal religion are, *de facto, members of an invisible race of men and women* metaphorically referred to as the White Brotherhood. They are *invisible*, not because they do not occupy physical bodies with varying degrees of skin pigmentation, which they do, but rather because they are recognizable only with the inner eye of character and wholeness, and not with the physical eye of particulars, distinction, and separateness. Members of this "invisible race" recognize each other only through the nature and clarity of their character and are truly members of what may be called *the new race of humanity whose love for all that is,* transcends common understanding."

The Templar endeavors to be an embodiment of this new spiritual race that is being born in greater numbers at this time- because there is a need for its manifestation to deal with the problems that humanity has created for itself in the world.

In some traditional legends, the Grail is represented by an emerald, which is an allusion to the "emerald tablet" of Hermes, and the astral source that the Templar must work with. The Templar must recognize that all manner of psychological disorders and unbalanced manifestations come from attachment and obsessive desire for the illusion of physical needs. The Templar cannot be rooted in these things. Rather, the Templar must keep their consciousness rooted in the spiritual source behind manifestations, and endeavor to gain wisdom from them- especially in situations that are the most challenging.

We have gone through different astrological cycles, or ages, and with each age new energies are introduced to the human consciousness. For the last 2000 years we have been in the Age of Pisces, whose astrological symbol is two fish swimming in opposite directions. This represents the age of discrimination for the Piscean Age, in which everything was either black- or white, good or evil, conservative or liberal, scientific or religious... Duality defined people during this age!

We are now going into the Age of Aquarius- the Vessel Carrier, whose symbol is two streams flowing together, and is representative of the Grail and the Grail Maiden. Duality is still present, but it is working synergistically. Things don't have to be this way *or* that way, but rather this way *and* that way. The Templar must be able to find this middle term that connects all *apparent* opposites. All apparent extremes are just degrees of the same consciousness. Where does "hot" begin and "cold" end? Both are extremes of a thing we call "temperature", and both can be utilized for the good of different situations and needs. The Templar must be open to seeing how different things and perspectives can be utilized, without projecting his or her own personal insecurities and/or cultural conditioning onto the situation that may be at hand. Science and spirituality can be reconciled through the study of consciousness and how it manifests- to give only one example of a reconciliation which will become important in the age to come. Unity expresses through opposition to itself!

The Templar can help to foster the creation of a better world, but must first find the reconciliation within, in order to do it. *As within, so without*! The coming age is a balanced age, where the masculine and feminine energies must work together in mutual support, and appreciation of each other's mutual strengths. This may manifest in strange ways at first, but in the end, these energies will become balanced within each individual, and all people can come to wholeness. A study of Carl Jung is encouraged in this regard.

The Hemetic philosophers recognized a profound truth, which is that the only way The Creator of All could have created, is within

His own Mind- since there was nothing outside of Him prior to creation. Therefore, everything we see and think is real and solid and tangible, is actually just the consciousness "mind stuff" of the Creator, within His mind. Therefore the Creator must be achieving greater levels of awakening through our actions and our personal awakening! Personally awakening to this realization provides the power that the Templar needs to be a co-Creator in creation itself. Therefore the Templar can be the alchemist in the world, transmuting his/her own base self into something precious first, and thereby helping to transmute the world as a whole around him or her. Transmutation and awakening heals the wasteland. The Templar connects and transmutes *through the bonds of spiritual chivalry*...

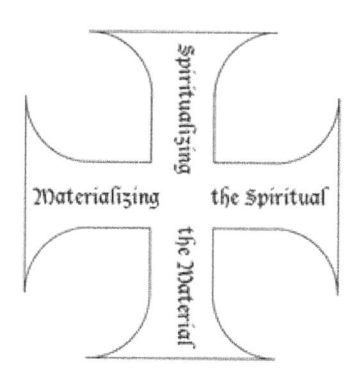

Materializing — *the Spiritual*

Spiritualizing — *the Material*

100

X. Templar Ideas to Remember

There are some fundamental ideas that we can learn from the history of the Templar tradition, which comes from their mission, philosophy, and works, and which have come down to us from 1096 to the present day, and which allow us to live *in the bonds of spiritual chivalry*. Any Templar, of any lineage, should meditate on the ideas outlined below, which are developed perspectives from the tradition itself:

1) Hate is almost always a product of cultural conditioning. If you hate ANY group of people, you need to ask yourself, who had an agenda to teach you to hate those other people and why? It usually always goes back to something as petty as economic gain for somebody other than you! It is always better, and it takes more inner conviction, to think with your own heart, rather than to blindly follow somebody else's agenda for you- which makes you their unknowing slave... The True Impulses of the human soul does not know hate, and cannot know hate, because the true source of the human soul is connected to everyone else. This is the foundation of true freedom!

2) We will begin to remember our past incarnations as soon as we are willing to step up and live authentically in this incarnation. Living authentically means being an expression of the promptings of your soul- your true self, your true "higher nature", even when our loved ones will persecute us for being an expression of such truth. The access of higher memory is only available to those who are willing to be an expression of a higher life-without living from fear. It is a temporary blessing, however, that God

makes most forget their past, as remembering our past forces us to acknowledge what we have been, and how our past personalities have expressed. It can be painful to see and acknowledge how far we have fallen short in the past- and how we must ask forgiveness to God for our past trespasses before moving forward to new levels of awakening. Denial is the root of all forgetfulness.

3) It is a blessing to spend time with wonderful people, who in turn enrich, empower, and give greater meaning to your incarnation. When you find such people, you have one of the greatest gifts that God can manifest. Appreciate them as a treasure, and never take them for granted. Give back to them as much as they give to you, in whatever way your personal gifts and talents can. In doing this, a bond is formed that brings us all closer to our Source! Try to inspire all people to become wonderful...

4) Whatever you do...make it meaningful!

5) Many fears ARE born from loneliness and fatigue, and you are vulnerable to being used by others when you are in this state. Best case scenario, others in the same state will try to use you to justify their own fears. Worst case scenario, you will be manipulated by others to support their own political agenda- which in the end, there is always someone profiting off of financially. Go take a nap or rest in the silence of meditation, and know that you are loved! The world is not as bad as the lonely, vulnerable people make it sound like it is. Don't get too caught up in sensationalized drama. When someone asks you to be afraid, they are really asking you to give your power away

to them. A Templar can stand firm even when attacked, as a Templar carries within the Peace of God.

6) Every time we define something, we are recreating it. Be careful with your words and expressive reactions. Define the world that should be, and don't get caught putting energy into the drama of the way the world has been. Your words are your sword of light, which protects the symbolic Eden, from which you never should have fallen!

7) Let us hope the Truth speaks for itself and is not being used as a tool for sectarian motives! Thus during the Age of Taurus we find Isis-Hathor in Egypt- with her bull horns, from which comes the golden calf. In the Age of Aries we find the priesthood as Shepherds in the Old Testament/Torah, and we see the Legends of the Golden Fleece in Greece, and even Moses as depicted with horns! Even the Egyptian god Amon is depicted as a ram... In Pisces we see the advent of Christianity and new symbolic fishermen leaders. The early Christian symbol was a vesica pisces, or fish, for this reason. We begin our tradition into the Age of Aquarius- the vessel carrier...the Grail... As the Master Jesus said, "Behold, when you have entered the city, a man will meet you carrying a vessel of water; follow him into the house which he enters..." So must we go likewise to the Last Supper and partake in the alchemical communion of Melchizedek!

8) 2000 years ago the Master Jesus never worshiped *The Creator* under the German derived name of "God". Therefore it is hypocritical for any modern so-called "Christian" to criticize others for worshiping The Creator under names other than "God". Let this lesson be heard by

people of all religions: It is not the name of the Creator that matters so much, from whatever language or religion, but more importantly the intent behind the prayer itself that does matter... The Creator will respond to you by whatever name you address Him by- if your heart is full of pure intent.

9) The Templar Masters understand that even when people ride your coat tails to an amazing place that you take them, many will still complain about the bumpy ride... People will see and appreciate based on where they are at internally, and you have to be fine with that...encouraging them to see the beauty that is around them and within them.

10) When the Templar Master is done acting, the masses will project their hopes and fears onto him/her depending on their level of security with themselves. Those who are truly striving for Mastery however, will recognize that the Master's actions stemmed from the same source that is within themselves, for every Master is just a working tool of God.

11) The goal of the Templar is to ceaselessly work to transform every situation that they encounter in their life from lead into gold; the goal of the profane is relish in their attachment and false dependence on lead... Those who live for lead, die with lead; those who strive to turn lead into gold have created a golden life for themselves and others.

12) Do not fight for a Holy Land on earth, for you will destroy the true Holy Land within...

13) In order to achieve the Grail, one must become the Grail. In so doing, one will have the blessing of Melchizadek. One

will witness the second coming of the Christos. One becomes the living embodiment of the Paraclete. One will freely give the Grail to others, *if their heart is open to receiving it*.

14) We are One human family, in the One Mind of the One Creator. Even those who are not "human" are part of this same One Thing, and are striving, whether they are aware of it or not, to be connected to it. Those who have awakened to the One are responsible for bringing those who haven't awakened to the One back to the One.

15) All great Masters are manifestations of the same Master.

16) It is not enough to just observe. One must also participate- even if participating just involves sending positive thoughts of love and healing. Let your actions be your prayer. Your work is your worship!

17) How you present yourself in the world is a reflection of how you want the world to be. Aspire towards greater levels of Unity, cooperation and love. Set a higher standard to strive to in the world. Do not be content with mundane and profane expressions of consciousness manifestation. Be the expression of One Love!

18) When this life is over, what will be remembered, retained, and passed on for ourselves and others, is the positive manifestations we endeavored to create. No memorization of so called facts or knowledge is carried with us. Only what we have done with such things matters.

19) Be open to possibility!

XI. Templar Collegia Proclamation

Be it known to all of disciplined mind and chivalrous heart that the time has once again come to don the armor of self-knowledge and extract from the Stone of the Philosophers the sword of justice, peace, and love; to unite once again as Knights in defense of all that is Holy, virtuous and good, and to affirm all that is positive and constructive in human society, be it of the individual or of the collectivity, without regard to gender, race, economic or social status, religious or political persuasion. The time has once again come for the Portals of the Order of the Temple to be opened to those who feel that inner yearning; to those who thirst for divine and inner wholeness remains unquenched. The signal has been given that you who have labored long and hard in the vineyard of the Master; you who have long practiced the esoteric principles of self-discipline; you who have felt the inner calling and have roamed the desert of outer understanding in quest of a resting place, an oasis of inner calm, the time has come for you to bring to the table of humanity your special gift so that those who hunger and thirst may partake and sip from the Grail of the Temple and live; so that in their partaking and in your sharing, you too may receive the armor of self-knowledge and your sword of chivalry. Never before in the history of humanity has the need for the opening of the portals of the Sovereign Order of the Initiatic Temple been greater. Heed the call and contribute to the evolution of humanity!

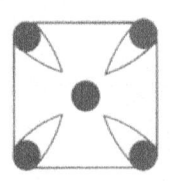

XII. Recommended Reading and Sources Mentioned in this Book

Bernard, Raymond, *A Secret Meeting in Rome*, Lulu, 2012.

Butler, Alan & Stephan Dafoe, *The Warriors and the Bankers*, Lewis Masonic, UK, 2010.

Charpentier, Louis, *The Mysteries of Chartres Cathedral*, translated by Sir Ronald Fraser, RILKO Books, Athenaeum Press, Sussex, 2002.

Chrétien De Troyes, *Perceval Ou Le Roman Du Graal*, translation by Jean-Pierre-Foucher and Andre Ortais, Paris, 1974.

Dawkins, Peter, *Studies in Ancient Wisdom: Dedication to the Light: The Bardic Mysteries, The Love Affair of Elizabeth I and Leicester, The Birth and Adoption of Francis Bacon*, Francis Bacon Research Trust, England, 1988.

Fulcanelli, *Le Mystere des Cathedrales*, translated by Mary Sworder, Brotherhood of Life, Inc., 2000.

Hall, Manly Palmer, *Orders of the Quest: The Holy Grail*, Philosophical Research Society, Los Angeles, 1949.

Herd, Robert, *The Initiatic Experience*, Starr Publishing, Colorado, 2012.

Hogan, Timothy, *Entering the Chain of Union*, Lulu, 2011.

HRH Prince Michael of Albany and Walid Amine Salhab, *The Knights Templar of the Middle East*, Weiser Books, San Francisco, 2006.

King, C.W., *The Gnostics and Their Remains, Ancient and Medieval*, William Clowes and Sons, London, 1887.

Koussa, Karim El, *Jesus the Phoenician*, Sunbury Press, PA, 2013

Levi, Eliphas, *Unpublished Letters of Eliphas Levi*, L'Initiation- Vols. 9 and 10, 1890-91.

Mitchell, Thomas J., *Rosslyn Chapel: The Music of the Cubes*, Diversions, UK, 2006.

Official Ritual: Heredom of Kilwinning and Rosy Cross, Grand Lodge of the Royal Order of Scotland, Edinburgh, 1998.

Picknett, Lynn and Prince, Clive, *The Templar Revelation*, Touchstone, New York, 1997.

Pike, Albert, *Morals and Dogma*, The Supreme Council of Southern Jurisdiction, Charleston, 1906.

Robinson, *John J., Born In Blood*, M.Evans & Company, New York, 1989.

Wilson, Onslow, *Psyche's Secret: The Path of Personal Integration, A HealQuest Trilogy- Volume 1,* Raoma Publication, Indiana, 2008.

Wolfram von Eschenbach, *Parzival*, Translated by A. T. Hatto, Penguin, London, 1980.

Made in the USA
Coppell, TX
26 July 2020